"十一五"国家重点出版规划项目
全国高职高专公共英语教材

总顾问 ◎ 胡壮麟　孙亦丽
总主编 ◎ 丁国声

新世纪交际
英语教程 ①
（修订版）
学生用书

全国高职高专公共英语教材编写组　编
邓仕伦　罗道茂　主　编

图书在版编目(CIP)数据

新世纪交际英语教程(1)学生用书/全国高职高专公共英语教材编写组编;邓仕伦,罗道茂主编.—2版(修订本).—北京:北京大学出版社,2010.1
(全国高职高专公共英语教材)
ISBN 978-7-301-16871-4

Ⅰ.新…　Ⅱ.①全…②邓…③罗…　Ⅲ.英语-高等学校:技术学校-教材　Ⅳ.H31

中国版本图书馆CIP数据核字(2010)第005103号

书　　　名:新世纪交际英语教程(1)学生用书(修订版)
著作责任者:全国高职高专公共英语教材编写组　编　邓仕伦　罗道茂　主编
策　　　划:张冰　李颖
责 任 编 辑:李颖
标 准 书 号:ISBN 978-7-301-16871-4/H·2409
出 版 发 行:北京大学出版社
地　　　址:北京市海淀区成府路205号　100871
网　　　址:http://www.pup.cn
电　　　话:邮购部 62752015　发行部 62750672　编辑部 62755217　出版部 62754962
电 子 邮 箱:zbing@pup.pku.edu.cn
印　刷　者:北京大学印刷厂
经　销　者:新华书店
　　　　　787毫米×1092毫米　16开本　8印张　184千字
　　　　　2006年5月第1版　2010年1月第2版
　　　　　2014年1月第7次印刷
定　　　价:20.00元(配有光盘)

未经许可,不得以任何方式复制或抄袭本书之部分或全部内容。
版权所有,侵权必究　　举报电话:010-62752024
　　　　　　　　　　　电子邮箱:fd@pup.pku.edu.cn

总顾问　胡壮麟　孙亦丽
总主编　丁国声

主　编　邓仕伦　罗道茂

编　者（以姓氏笔画为序）
　　　　马玉玲　　王永斌　　李义容　　李建群　　刘　忠
　　　　刘杰伟　　刘　静　　刘　嘉　　邢莉娟　　伏　伟
　　　　杨　樱　　张　红　　欧昌清　　郑翠兰　　阎晓玲

总　序

近年来,高等职业教育的发展规模迅速扩大,形成了"半分天下",为中国的大众化高等教育做出了重要贡献。随着规模发展,一系列的教育质量工程陆续展开。其中,规划教材和精品教材的评选均旨在提高教学水平。教改的关键是教师,教师的关键是教材,教材的关键是理念。

高职的教材建设虽然与教育快速发展现状之间的差距在缩小,但在教材建设方面仍然缺乏规划和标准,在使用和出版方面存在随意性和功利性。因此,适合高职培养目标和紧贴市场需求的高水准的教材少之又少。当务之急是认真抓好高职教材编写队伍建设,增强教材建设的精品意识,使教材的编写出版符合职业教育的规律。

高职教材可分为两大类,即文化基础课教材和专业基础课教材。北京大学出版社出版的《新世纪应用英语教程》和《新世纪交际英语教程》是一套文化基础课教材。这次修订教材的目的是使其教材定位准确、模式科学、质量上乘和内容新颖。经过编写人员的努力,新修订的教材终于焕然一新、与时俱进,反映出了高职教育的改革思路。高职教育在改革摸索,教材编写在开发探讨。希望更多的像北京大学出版社这样的权威知名机构积极关心和参与高职教育的改革和发展,使高职教育真正走上由规模发展转向质量发展的健康之路。

丁国声

全国高职高专公共英语教材　总主编
教育部高等学校高职高专英语类专业教学指导委员会　委　员
河北外国语职业学院　院　长

前　言

　　《全国高职高专公共英语教材》是为进一步落实国家《2003—2007年教育振兴行动计划》，在广泛调研的基础上依据教育部《高职高专教育英语课程教学基本要求》(以下简称《基本要求》)特为全国高职高专非英语专业学生编写的一套公共英语教材，并被列入"十一五"国家重点出版规划项目《面向新世纪的立体化网络化英语学科建设丛书》。本套教材取材丰富，题材多样，贴近生活，时代感强，是一套集应用性、实用性、趣味性和文化性为一体的特色英语教科书。为方便学生学习和教学安排，本教材分为两大体系：新世纪应用英语教程(着重于读、写、译)和新世纪交际英语教程(着重于视、听、说)。这两大体系既相照应又相包容，不仅使听、说、读、写、译五大语言基本技能训练得到有效的整合，并科学地贯穿于英语教学的全过程，而且还从不同的角度为学生的语言学习提供生动多元的文化氛围和真实丰富的语言环境，从而使语言学习、语言实践、语言应用以及文化体验有机结合，十分有利于学生语言应用能力的培养与提高。

　　本教材为《新世纪交际英语教程》，在编写过程中充分吸收各种现有教材的优点并努力创新，形成了如下主要特色：

　　构思独特　　在借鉴其他同类教材编排体系优点的基础上，本教材充分考虑现代教育技术在英语教学中的应用，把视、听、说融为一体，每一部分(Unit)都设计一个"视听"小节(Section)。通过"影视"的辅助作用强化学生的听说能力，同时也提高学生的学习兴趣。

　　实用性强　　考虑到高职高专学生的实际需要，本教材尤其突出教学材料的实用性，即充分注意高职高专学生学时少、职业培训倾向性强的特点；同时，本教材还努力选用一些贴近高校学生生活的材料，提高学生的学习积极性。

　　选材新颖　　全书语言材料大部分选自英文原文，编者主要利用网络、新近出版的外国原版书籍、杂志、小册子等进行材料筛选，最终交付主编审定；这些材料一方面内容贴近当代生活，时代感强，容易激发学生的学习热情；另一方面在语言上比较活泼，容易引发学生兴趣；此外，熟悉这些材料，有利于学生了解当代社会生活，对他们毕业后很快适应工作需要极有帮助。

　　循序渐进　　本教材在语法知识、语汇、句法、语速等方面，在大量语料分析的前提下,严格按照从易到难进行教学。

　　总之,本教材具有较强的思想性、科学性、知识性、趣味性;语言规范,体系性强,练习兼具实用性和针对性,使学生真正做到看得懂、听得懂、说得出、用得活,为将来的英语学习及在工作中使用英语打下坚实的基础。本教材配备多媒体网络系统和电子课件;提供图文、声音、视频等传统教程难以提供的多方位的学习资料;提供学生的个性化学习平台;提供教学内容的持续更新和动态扩展。

　　本系列教材具有高品位和权威性,由北京大学在文科享受两院院士级待遇的资深教授胡壮麟先生担任总顾问、北京大学英语系教授孙亦丽先生担任总主编,北京交通大学、重庆大学、成都大学等教学科研第一线的骨干教师参与编写工作。本书承外籍教授 Pauline.Emily 审阅并提出宝贵修改意见。北京大学出版社为本教材的出版做了大量的工作。编者在此向他们表示真诚的感谢。同时,对以上参编单位的领导的大力支持也表示衷心的谢意。

2005 年 10 月

Unit One

Greetings and Introductions ·········· 1

Part I   Phonetics ·········· 1
Part II Dialogues ·········· 4
Part III Passages ·········· 7
Part IV Oral Practice ·········· 10
Part V   Learn to Sing a Song ·········· 13

Unit Two

Asking the Way ·········· 14

Part I   Phonetics ·········· 14
Part II Dialogues ·········· 17
Part III Passages ·········· 21
Part IV Oral Practice ·········· 23
Part V   Learn to Sing a Song ·········· 25

Unit Three

Offering Help ·········· 27

Part I   Phonetics ·········· 27
Part II Dialogues ·········· 30
Part III Passages ·········· 33
Part IV Oral Practice ·········· 35
Part V   Learn to Sing a Song ·········· 38

Unit Four

Shopping ·········· 39

Part I   Phonetics ·········· 39
Part II Dialogues ·········· 42
Part III Passages ·········· 45

Part IV Oral Practice ·· 47
Part V   Learn to Sing a Song ································· 51

Unit Five
Apologies ·· 53
Part I   Cardinals ·· 53
Part II   Dialogues ·· 57
Part III Passages ·· 61
Part IV   Oral Practice ·· 63
Part V   Learn to Sing a Song ································ 66

Unit Six
Going to a Party ·································· 67
Part I   Ordinals ·· 67
Part II   Dialogues ·· 70
Part III Passages ·· 73
Part IV   Oral Practice ·· 75
Part V   Learn to Sing a Song ································ 79

Unit Seven
Seeing the Doctor ································ 80
Part I   Teen's and Ten's ······································ 80
Part II   Dialogues ·· 83
Part III Passages ·· 86
Part IV   Oral Practice ·· 88
Part V   Learn to Sing a Song ································ 92

Unit Eight
A Job Interview 93
Part I General Questions and Special Questions 93
Part II Dialogues 96
Part III Passages 99
Part IV Oral Practice 101
Part V Learn to Sing a Song 105

Vocabulary 106

UNIT ONE

Greetings and Introductions

Part 1 Phonetics

Phonetic Practice:

/iː/	/ɪ/	/æ/	/e/	/əː/	/ə/
/ʌ/	/ɔː/	/ɔ/	/uː/	/ʊ/	/ɑː/

1. Listen and repeat the following words, pay attention to the colored parts.

(1) /iː/	we	meet	believe	seat	people
(2) /ɪ/	English	interest	kid	system	village
(3) /æ/	map	have	man	language	matter
(4) /e/	question	help	men	when	ready
(5) /əː/	person	girl	word	burn	learn

(6) /ə/	teacher	future	author	around	problem
(7) /ʌ/	fun	come	courage	trouble	above
(8) /ɔː/	August	floor	talk	law	report
(9) /ɔ/	on	lot	doctor	quality	want
(10) /uː/	school	true	through	June	you
(11) /ʊ/	good	book	look	put	would
(12) /ɑː/	star	mark	heart	ask	half

 2. Listen to the poem written by Percy Bysshe Shelley "A Song." Choose the words you hear to fill in the blanks.

New Words

sate	/seɪt/	v.	使心满意足, 过分地给与
mourning	/ˈmɔːnɪŋ/	n.	悲恸, 服丧
wintry	/ˈwɪntrɪ/	a.	像冬季的, 寒冷的, 冬天的, 冷淡的
freeze	/friːz/	v.	(使)结冰, (使)冷冻, 冻结
crept	/krept/		creep 的过去式
creep	/kriːp/	v.	爬, 蹑手蹑脚, 蔓延
bare	/bɛə/	a.	赤裸的, 无遮蔽的, 空的
		v.	使赤裸, 露出

Poem

A SONG

Percy Bysshe Shelley

A _____ (widow, wonder) bird sate mourning for her love
　　　　Upon a wintry _____ (bore, bough);
The frozen _____ (wand, wind) crept on above
　　　　The freezing stream _____ (below, belie).
There was no _____ (life, leaf) upon the forest bare,
　　　　No flower upon the _____ (grand, ground),
And little _____ (mission, motion) in the air
　　　　Except the mill-wheel's _____ (sound, sand).

3. Read aloud the poem sentence by sentence after the speaker.

4. Practice the tongue twister sentence by sentence after the speaker. Pay attention to the sounds.

   (1) Cat, cat catches a fat rat.

   (2) A big black bug bit a big black bear and made the big black bear bleed blood.

   (3) She sells sea shells on the seashore. The seashells she sells are seashells she is sure.

Part II Dialogues

Warming Up

Greetings

(1) —How do you do?

—How do you do?

(2) —How are you? /How are you getting along with your work? /How are things going with you? /How are you doing?

—Fine/Very well/Not bad/All right, thank you. And you?

—Fine/Very well/Not bad/All right, thanks.

(3) —Hello/Hi, beautiful day, isn't it?

—Yes, it is.

(4) —Good morning/afternoon/evening.

—Good morning/afternoon/evening.

(5) —Nice to meet you.

—Nice to meet you, too.

(6) —Haven't seen you for a long time.

—Fancy meeting you here.

Introducing yourself

(1) May I introduce myself? My name is...

(2) Could I say a few words about myself?

(3) Let me introduce myself. I'm... My major is...

(4) Let me tell you something about myself.

(5) Allow me to introduce myself.

Introducing someone else

(1) May I introduce Professor Wang to you?

(2) I'd like to introduce my friend, an American visiting scholar to you.

(3) I'd like you to meet Mr. Wang, my English teacher.

(4) Let me introduce my classmate Miss Li to you.

(5) This is Professor Wilson. He is from America.

(6) Allow me to introduce Miss White to you.

1. **Video: Watch the video and do the activities as indicated.**

New Words and Expressions

convent	/'kɔnvənt/	n.	女修道会,女修道院
governess	/'gʌvənɪs/	n.	女家庭教师
butler	/'bʌtlə/	n.	仆役长,男管家
abbey	/'æbɪ/	n.	修道院;[总称]修道士
maintain	/meɪn'teɪn/	v.	维持;继续;供养;主张
discipline	/'dɪsɪplɪn/	n.	纪律;学科
drill	/drɪl/	v.	训练;钻孔;条播(种子)
utmost	/'ʌtməust/	a.	极度的;最远的
decorum	/dɪ'kɔːrəm/	n.	礼貌
humiliating	/hjuː'mɪlieɪtɪŋ/	a.	羞辱性的
incorrigible	/ɪn'kɔrɪdʒəbl/	a.	无药可救的,不能被纠正的
parasol	/ˌpærə'sɔl, 'pærəsɔl/	n.	(女用)阳伞

Activities

(1) Try to use your own words to explain what you have seen in the video.

(2) What do you think of the Captain?

(3) What do you think is the most important thing for you to learn? Why?

2. Listen to the following short dialogues and fill in the blanks with the information you get from the tape. Each dialogue will be read twice.

(1) W: _____. Mr. Davis. I'm glad you could come. It's nice to see you again.

   M: Hello, Miss Sally. _____.

(2) W: Good heavens... Peter! _____.

   M: I've been away for the past two months. _____?

   W: Very well, thanks.

(3) W: Glad to see you again, Bill. I hope _____.

   M: _____, thank you.

(4) M: Barbara, this is the person _____, John MacDonald.

   W: Hello, John, _____. Tom has told me all about you already.

(5) W: Excuse me, are you John Smith?

   M: Yes, I am. You must be Miss Brown.

W: Yes, I am Mary Brown. My boss asked me to meet you.

M: That is _____. Thank you.

3. You will hear 5 recorded questions. Listen carefully and choose the proper answer to each question. The questions will be spoken twice.

(1) A. Good, I will be free then.　　B. Yes, I'd love to.
　　C. How are you?　　D. How do you do?

(2) A. I live in the city.　　B. I am from the library.
　　C. Oh, thank you.　　D. I am from Canada.

(3) A. How are you?　　B. How are you going?
　　C. Fine, too.　　D. Hello.

(4) A. Yes, I look pale.　　B. I've got a headache.
　　C. Nor am I.　　D. Don't mention it.

(5) A. I'm very well.　　B. I've done it before.
　　C. It sounds good!　　D. I'm a doctor.

Part III Passages

1. Listen to the passage and supply the missing words. It will be read three times.

1　　　A pleasant _____ to people is a form of good manners. It adds to life's happiness. It is pleasant to receive a _____, a bend of the head or a spoken greeting as one walks along the street, and it is surprising what a chill (寒心) it gives one when such a greeting is unnoticed. Failure to greet a person or to _____ a greeting given to you is unkindness to the other person. And it is a bad manner.

2   The simple thing to say is "Good morning," "Good afternoon," or "Good evening." This greeting is given to one who you know _____ slightly, or to anyone you are passing quickly. "How do you do?" is usually _____ when you meet someone for the first time. No answer is expected other _____ "How do you do?" "How are you?" sometimes is just a form of politeness, and should be replied to you "Fine, thank you."?

3   Some forms of greeting which are good manners in China are not used in the _____. If you should greet a westerner by saying "Where are you going?" or "Where have you been?" he or she would think you were not polite to ask about his or her _____ affairs. And if you should say "Have you had your dinner?" he or she would think you were going to _____ him or her to have dinner with you. So it is better to use a usual Western form for greeting.

2. Listen to the passage again and answer the following questions.

(1) What does a pleasant greeting to people add to?

(2) What is bad manners according to the speaker?

(3) What should you say when you meet someone for the first time?

(4) Are all the forms of greeting in China the same as in the West?

(5) Can you greet a Westerner with "Have you had your dinner"? Why?

3. Listen to a passage twice and decide whether the following statements are true (T) or false (F).

___ (1) When the small boy and his father were walking in the country, they took an umbrella with them.

___ (2) When it rained very hard, they were soon very wet, because the umbrella was unable to cover them.

___ (3) The boy was very happy while it was raining so hard.

___ (4) The boy's father said the rain is very useful and explained its benefit.

___ (5) The boy still doubted about the benefit of the rain.

4. Watch the video and enjoy the movie clip.

New Words

syllabus	/ˈsɪləbəs/	n.	课程提纲
presume	/prɪˈzjuːm/	v.	假定,假设,认为
impulse	/ˈɪmpʌls/	n.	推动,推动力;刺激;冲动
sophisticated	/səˈfɪstɪkeɪtɪd/	a.	诡辩的;久经世故的
hump	/hʌmp/	n.	驼峰,驼背;小圆丘,峰丘
archeologists	/ˌɑːkɪˈɔlədʒɪst/	n.	考古学家
depict	/dɪˈpɪkt/	v.	描述,描写
primitive	/ˈprɪmɪtɪv/	a.	原始的,远古的;粗糙的;简单的
funerary	/ˈfjuːnərərɪ/	a.	葬礼的,埋葬的
pharaoh	/ˈfɛərəʊ/	n.	法老(古埃及君主称号);暴君
supplement	/ˈsʌplɪmənt/	n.	补遗,补充;附录,增刊

Part IV Oral Practice

Text A

Tom and Mary are friends but haven't seen each other for a long time. They meet again now.

Tom: Hi, Mary. I haven't seen you for ages. How is everything with you?

Mary: Not bad, Tom, thanks, and you?

Tom: Fine, thank you. Well, how is your brother?

Mary: Great. My brother is now studying in Chongqing Electronics Polytechnic College. A freshman, you know.

Tom: How is he getting on with his study?

Mary: Quite well. He loves his major and works hard on it.

Tom: By the way, what does he major in?

Mary: Computer science.

Tom: Really? Could you tell me how to contact him? I like computer, too, and maybe I can learn something from your brother.

Mary: His telephone number is 651-234-987.

Tom: Thanks a lot.

Mary: You're welcome, Tom. Good-bye.

Tom: Good-bye, Mary.

Text B

Mr. Brown and Miss White come to China on business. They are now meeting their Chinese partners.

Mr. Zhang: Good afternoon, Mr. Brown. Welcome to our company.

Mr. Brown:	Good afternoon, Mr. Zhang. Let me introduce our marketing manager, Miss White, to you.
Mr. Zhang:	How do you do, Miss White? I'm glad to meet you.
Miss White:	How do you do? Very glad to meet you, too.
Mr. Zhang:	I'd like you to know my colleague, Miss Wang. Miss Wang, this is Miss White, and this is Mr. Brown.
Miss White and Mr. Brown:	Nice to meet you, Miss Wang.
Miss Wang:	Nice to meet you, too. Welcome to China.
Mr. Zhang:	Take a seat, please. What would you like to drink?
Miss White:	I'd like some coffee, please.
Mr. Brown:	Tea, please.
Miss Wang:	Did you have a nice trip?
Mr. Brown:	We enjoyed the trip, thank you.
Miss Wang:	We hope you'll also enjoy your stay here.
Miss White:	I think we will. Thank you.

New Words and Expressions

freshman	/ˈfreʃmən/	n.	新生,大学一年级学生
major	/ˈmeɪdʒə/	v.	主修
partner	/ˈpɑːtnə/	n.	合伙人,股东
colleague	/ˈkɔliːg/	n.	同事,同僚
by the way			顺便说一下
major in			主修,专攻
on business			(因公)出差
marketing manager			市场营销部经理

Proper Names

Chongqing Electronics Polytechnic College		重庆电子职业技术学院
Tom	/tɔm/	汤姆（男子名）
Mary	/'mɛərɪ/	玛丽（女子名）
Brown	/braʊn/	布朗（姓氏）
White	/(h)waɪt/	怀特（姓氏）

Task Role Play

Students act as Mary and Tom or Miss White, Mr. Brown, Miss Wang and Mr. Zhang. Act out Text A or Text B.

Exercises

(1) Today is the first day of the new term. Now you and your deskmate introduce yourselves to each other. Please make up a dialogue.

Useful Words and Expressions

Hello!	你好！
My name is...	我叫……
Where are you from?	你从什么地方来？
I'd like you to meet...	我想请你见见……
It's nice to meet you.	很高兴见到你。

(2) Imagine you are meeting Mr. Tom Johnson, a foreign guest from Canada, at the airport. Make up a dialogue, exchanging greetings.

Useful Words and Expressions

Excuse me.	劳驾/对不起。
How do you do?	你好！
Welcome to...	欢迎来到……

It's a pleasure to meet you.　　很高兴见到你。
This way, please.　　　　　　　这边请。

Part V　Learn to Sing a Song

 1. Listen to the song "Ding Dong Bell."

 2. Listen to the song again and fill in the missing words.

Ding Dong Bell

Ding dong bell. Pussy's in the _____. Who put her in? Little Donny Green.　Who pulled her _____? Little Tommy stout.　What a _____ boy was that to drown _____ pussy cat,　who never did any harm but killed all the _____ on his father farm.

3. Learn to sing the song after the singer.

UNIT TWO

Asking the Way

Part 1   Phonetics

Phonetic Practice:

| /eɪ/ | /aɪ/ | /aʊ/ | /əʊ/ |
| /ɔɪ/ | /ɪə/ | /ɛə/ | /ʊə/ |

 1. Listen and repeat the following words, pay attention to the colored parts.

(1) /eɪ/	eight	age	late	train	cake
(2) /aɪ/	fine	sky	kite	ice	either
(3) /aʊ/	house	brown	out	shout	ground
(4) /əʊ/	own	only	cold	road	grow
(5) /ɔɪ/	noise	toy	coin	boy	voice

14

(6) /ɪə/	dear	here	appear	beer	clear
(7) /ɛə/	care	bear	there	hair	swear
(8) /ʊə/	sure	poor	usual	tour	moor

2. Listen to the poem written by H. W. Longfellow "The Arrow and the Song." Choose the words you hear to fill in the blanks.

New Words

arrow	/ˈærəʊ/	n.	箭;箭头记号
swiftly	/ˈswɪftlɪ/	ad.	很快地,迅速地;即刻
breathe	/briːð/	v.	呼吸
follow	/ˈfɔləʊ/	v.	跟随
sight	/saɪt/	n.	视力,视线
oak	/əʊk/	n.	橡树

Poem

The Arrow and the Song

H. W. Longfellow

I _____ (shot, shoot) an arrow into the air,

It _____ (fill, fell) to earth, I know not where;

15

For, so swiftly it _____ (flew, flown), the sight

Could not follow its _____ (fight, flight).

I _____ (braced, breathed) a song into the air,

It fell to earth, I know not where;

For who has sight so _____ (keen, king) and strong,

That it can follow the flight of song.

Long, long _____ (afterwards, afterwords), in an oak,

I _____ (mind, found) the arrow, still unbroken;

And the song, from _____ (begun, beginning) to end,

I found again in the _____ (heat, heart) of a friend.

3. Read aloud the poem sentence by sentence after the speaker.

4. Practice the tongue twister sentence by sentence after the speaker. Pay attention to the sounds.

(1) There are thirty thousand feathers on that thrush's throat.

(2) Near an ear, a nearer ear, a nearly eerie ear.

(3) How much oil could a gum boil boil if a gum boil could boil oil?

Part II Dialogues

Warming Up

Asking the way

(1) —Can you tell / direct me where the post office is, please?

—Go straight to two blocks, turn right and it's on your right.

(2) —Excuse me. Could you tell me which way Hilton Hotel is?

—Yes, it's that way. You go three blocks, then turn left, it's opposite the post office.

(3) —Excuse me. I am looking for the Personnel Department.

—The Personnel Department isn't on this floor. It's on the fifth floor.

(4) —Excuse me. Can you tell me the way to the subway?

—Go straight along the road till you come to the corner. Then make a left turn.

(5) —Would you please tell me how to get to the sea?

—You should take the No. 1 tram.

1. Video: Watch the video and do the activities as indicated.

New Words and Expressions

pajamas	/pəˈdʒɑːməz/	n.	睡衣
cuff	/kʌf/	n.	袖口
fray	/freɪ/	v.	使磨损
dressy	/ˈdresɪ/	a.	衣着考究的
label	/ˈleɪbl/	n.	标签
commercial	/kəˈmɜːʃəl/	a.	商业的
wildly	/ˈwaɪldlɪ/	ad.	狂热地,野蛮地
dream	/driːm/	v.	梦想
dare	/dɛə/	v.	敢
absolutely	/ˈæbsəluːtlɪ/	ad.	完全地、绝对地
part	/pɑːt/	v.	分开
vicar	/ˈvɪkə/	n.	教区牧师
election	/ɪˈlekʃən/	n.	选举
Good luck!			祝你好运！
take a chance			冒险,碰运气

Proper Names

Liverpool Mercury		《利物浦信使报》
Keats	/kiːts/	济慈(1795—1821,英国诗人)

Activities

(1) Try to use your own words to explain what you have seen in the video.

(2) When and how is Smith supposed to come back home?

(3) Which train does Smith need to take?

(4) Where is the Liverpool Mercury Office?

(5) What is the important news in today's Liverpool Mercury?

2. **Listen to the following short dialogues and fill in the blanks with the information you get from the tape. Each dialogue will be read twice.**

(1) M: Excuse me. Can you _____ me to the First Department Store?

W: Yes, go straight ahead. It's on the right side of the street at the _____ traffic light.

(2) M: Is there a post office _____?

W: Well, let me see. It's not very far, but _____ complicated.

(3) M: Could you tell me where _____ is, please?

W: Certainly. It's _____, Room 318.

(4) M: Will you please tell me how to _____ the conference room?

W: Sure. Just go along the corridor there and turn right at the first right turning, then _____.

(5) M: Excuse me. Madam, I am _____ a petrol station.

　　W: Oh, I see. You are going in the _____.

(6) M: How _____ is it from here to the zoo?

　　W: Oh, you are _____ from it yet. It is about two kilometers from here.

3. You will hear 5 recorded questions. Listen carefully and choose the proper answer to each question. The questions will be spoken twice.

(1) A. Yes, it is the train station.　　　B. Yes, it will cost about $13.

　　C. Yes, it goes that direction.　　　D. Yes, it will take about 3 days by train.

(2) A. Sorry, I can't help you. I am new here.

　　B. No, you couldn't find any English book.

　　C. You no longer ask an English teacher.

　　D. Yes, you dislike English movie.

(3) A. Yes, it's 415 Fourth Street.　　　B. Yes, it's 514 Fifth Street.

　　C. Yes, it's 541 Fourth Street.　　　D. Yes, it's 415 Fifth Street.

(4) A. Yes, I have to work.　　　　　　B. Yes, I like to live far away.

　　C. No, it doesn't seem very far.　　D. No, I go to work by bus.

(5) A. No, I won't go to Xingya Restaurant.

　　B. Yes, I often eat in Xingya Restaurant.

　　C. Yes, I like the food served in Xingya Restaurant.

　　D. Sorry, I don't know how to get there.

Part III Passages

1. Listen to the passage and supply the missing words. It will be read three times.

1 Three months ago, Ms. Smith went to New York _____ her sister. It was the first time for her to come to New York. She did not know New York very well, and she _____ in the downtown area.

2 Suddenly, she saw an old man walking along a _____. She went to stop him and ask the way. "Excuse me," she said. "Could you tell me how to get to White Street, please?" The man looked _____. He did not understand English! He came from Spain and spoke Spanish. He was a traveler in New York. Then he put his right hand into his pocket and _____ a phrase book. He put on the glasses, opened the book and found a phrase. He read the phrase slowly. "I am sorry, Madam," he said. "I am a stranger here. I do not speak English."

2. Listen to the passage again and answer the following questions.

(1) When did Ms. Smith go to New York?

(2) Why did she go to New York?

(3) Which street did she want to go to?

(4) Whom did she stop to ask the way?

(5) Where did the man come from?

3. Listen to the passage and decide whether the following statements are true (T) or false (F).

___ (1) While waiting for the bus, I took out my collapsible white stick from my bag.

___ (2) The little girl wanted me to help her cross the street.

___ (3) I took the little girl to cross the street without any stop.

___ (4) We crossed the street safely.

___ (5) I took out my stick to make the return crossing after the sound of the little girl's steps died away.

4. Watch the video and enjoy the movie clip.

New Words

intelligent	/ɪnˈtelɪdʒənt/	a.	聪明的
sexy	/ˈseksɪ/	a.	性感的
live	/lɪv/	v.	过着，度过，经历
complicated	/ˈkɔmplɪkeɪtɪd/	a.	复杂的
leave alone			不打扰……
run away from			摆脱
as long as			只要

Proper Names

Angela	/ˈændʒɪlə/	n.	安吉拉(女子名)
Katrina	/kəˈtriːnə/	n.	卡特里娜(女子名)

Part IV Oral Practice

Text A

Bill stops a street vendor. He asks a vendor for directions.

Bill: Excuse me. Can you help me?
Vendor: Of course. What do you want?
Bill: Is 38 Nanjing Road near here?
Vendor: Yes, it is.
Bill: Could you tell me how to get there?
Vendor: That's easy. Walk to the corner. Then make a left turn. Then walk two blocks to the traffic lights.
Bill: Thank you very much.
Vendor: Don't mention it.

Text B

Mrs. Green is a tourist from the USA. After she walked around, she was puzzled and couldn't find the way to the People's Park. She is asking a policeman.

Mrs. Green: Excuse me. I'm a stranger here. Would you tell me where the People's Park is?
Policeman: The People's Park is located on Beijing Road, just on the opposite side of the International Conference and Exhibition Center.
Mrs. Green: How long will it take me to get there?
Policeman: Only about ten minutes.
Mrs. Green: I'm not going in the wrong direction, am I?
Policeman: No, you aren't. Just go straight ahead, please.

Mrs. Green: Can I take a bus to get there?
Policeman: Yes. You can take the No. 20 trolley bus to get there.
Mrs. Green: O.K. Thanks a lot.
Policeman: Not at all.

New Words and Expressions

vendor	/'vendɔː/	n.	卖主
puzzle	/'pʌzl/	v.	使迷惑
conference	/'kɔnfərəns/	n.	会议
trolley	/'trɔlɪ/	n.	电车
exhibition	/ˌeksɪ'bɪʃən/	n.	展览会
locate	/ləu'keɪt/	v.	坐落于

Proper Names

International Conference and Exhibition Center		国际会展中心
the People's Park		人民公园
Bill	/bɪl/	比尔(男子名, William 的昵称)
Green	/griːn/	格林(姓氏)

Task   Role Play

Students act as Bill and Vendor or Mrs. Green and Policeman. Act out Text A or Text B.

Exercises

(1) Imagine you are Nancy, a stranger in a city. You want to find a hotel, but you don't know your way around. Ask the policeman for directions according to the information given below.

Useful Expressions

block	/blɔk/	n.	街区
opposite	/ˈɔpəzit/	a.	对面的
direction	/dɪˈrekʃən/	n.	方向
transfer	/trænsˈfəː/	v.	换(车)
know one's way around			熟悉周围环境

(2) Suppose you are Li Ming. You are told to come to Personnel Department of the company to take an interview. You are asking the receptionist to show you the way to Personnel Department. Please make up a dialogue according to the information given below.

Useful Expressions

corridor	/ˈkɔridɔː/	n.	走廊
hall	/hɔːl/	n.	大厅
take the lift			乘电梯
guest room			会客室
Personnel Department			人事部

Part V Learn to Sing a Song

1. Listen to the song "Top of the World."

2. Listen to the song again and fill in the missing words.

Top of the World

Such a feeling's coming over me.　There is wonder in almost everything I see,　not a cloud _____ got the sun in my eyes and I won't be surprised if it's a dream. Everything I want the world to be is now _____ especially for me and the reason is clear. It's because you are here. You're the nearest thing to heaven that I've seen. I'm on the top of the world looking down on creation and the only explanation I can find is the love that I've found ever since you've been around. Your love's put me on the top of the world. _____ in the wind has learned my name and it's telling me that things are not the same in the leaves on the trees and the touch of the breeze. There's a pleasing sense of _____ for me. There is only one wish on my mind. When this day is through, I hope that I will find that tomorrow will be just the same for you and me.　All I _____ will be mine if you are here.　I'm on the top of the world looking down on creation and the only explanation I can find is the love that I've found ever since you've been around. Your love's put me on the top of the world.

3. Learn to sing the song after the singer.

UNIT THREE

Offering Help

Part 1 Phonetics

Phonetic Practice:

/p/	/b/	/t/	/d/	/k/	/g/	/f/	/v/
/s/	/z/	/θ/	/ð/	/ʃ/	/ʒ/	/r/	/h/
/m/	/n/	/ŋ/	/l/	/w/	/j/		

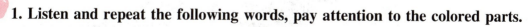

1. Listen and repeat the following words, pay attention to the colored parts.

(1) /p/   pass   park   happy   tape   map
(2) /b/   back   before   blank   table   cab
(3) /t/   ten   past   meet   tell   bet
(4) /d/   fade   tide   dig   down   today

(5) /k/	keep	cup	kill	coffee	back
(6) /g/	ground	gold	pig	colleague	ragged
(7) /f/	leaf	fee	laugh	photo	off
(8) /v/	vast	save	live	of	voice
(9) /s/	concert	ice	bus	listen	seat
(10) /z/	rise	zoo	prize	buzz	eyes
(11) /θ/	bath	north	thank	worth	thin
(12) /ð/	bathe	there	worthy	teethe	either
(13) /ʃ/	bush	shine	action	sheep	commercial
(14) /ʒ/	measure	usual	decision	occasion	garage
(15) /r/	read	wrong	write	crying	sorry
(16) /h/	hard	here	hat	have	behind
(17) /m/	warm	team	meet	mine	matter
(18) /n/	neat	turn	nine	in	man
(19) /ŋ/	sing	ring	song	wing	thing
(20) /l/	late	light	lead	luck	long
/l/	milk	help	call	girl	mile
(21) /w/	week	wife	web	sweet	wheel
(22) /j/	yes	year	young	yet	yellow

2. Listen to the poem "A Little Teapot." Choose the words you hear to fill in the blanks.

New Words

stout	/staʊt/	a.	结实的,健壮的
spout	/spaʊt/	n.	喷管,喷口,壶嘴
tip	/tɪp/	v.	(使)倾斜

Poem

A Little Teapot

Author Unknown

I'm a little teapot, _____ (short, stout) and _____ (stout, short)

Here is my _____ (hurdle, handle), here is my spout,

When the water's _____ (burning, boiling), hear me shout,

"Tip me over, _____ (pour, pull) me out!"

3. Read aloud the poem sentence by sentence after the speaker.

4. Practice the tongue twister sentence by sentence after the speaker. Pay attention to the sounds.

   (1) If I assist a sister-assistant, will the sister's sister-assistant assist me?

   (2) Peter Piper picked a peck of pickled peppers.

   A peck of pickled peppers Peter Piper picked.

   If Peter Piper picked a peck of pickled peppers,

   Where's the peck of pickled peppers Peter Piper picked?

   (3) a quick witted cricket critic

Part II Dialogues

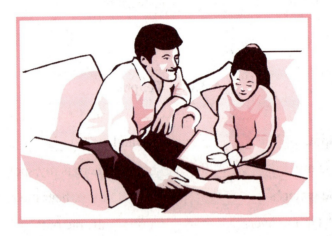

Warming Up

Offering something

(1) What can I do for you?

(2) Would you like me to set the table for you?

(3) What can I get you?

(4) Can I offer you something to eat?

(5) Is there anything I can do for you?

Accepting an offer of something

(1) Oh, please. Thanks a lot.

(2) If you would, please.

(3) Great.

(4) I'd be so pleased if you would.

(5) That would be very nice.

Declining an Offer of Something

(1) No, thanks.

(2) I won't, thanks.

(3) That's very kind, but I won't.

(4) Thanks for your offer, but I think I can manage.

(5) Not for me, thank you.

1. Video: Watch the video and do the activities as indicated.

New Words and Expressions

date	/deɪt/	v.	约会,定日期
kinda	/ˈkaɪndə/	ad.	(=kind of)有一点,有几分
moody	/ˈmuːdɪ/	a.	喜怒无常的,忧悒的
nephew	/ˈnefju(ː)/	n.	侄子,外甥
gonna	/ˈgɔnə/		[美] (=going to)将要
nuts	/nʌts/	a.	[美俚] 热衷的,发狂的
pie	/paɪ/	n.	馅饼
lime	/laɪm/	n.	酸橙
kiwi	/ˈkiːwiː/	n.	[植] 猕猴桃
allergic	/əˈləːdʒɪk/	a.	[医] 过敏的,患过敏症的
lobster	/ˈlɔbstə/	n.	龙虾
gotta	/ˈgɔtə/		[美俚] (=have got to)必须
wanna	/ˈwɔnə/	v.	[美俚] (= want to)想要,希望
diaper	/ˈdaɪəpə/	n.	尿布

Activities

(1) Try to use your own words to explain what you have seen in the video.

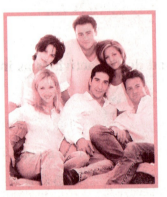

(2) What do you think of people in the video?

(3) What do you think is the most important thing for you to learn?

2. **Listen to the following short dialogues and fill in the blanks with the information you get from the tape. Each dialogue will be read twice.**

    (1) M: Excuse me, Mary, can I _____ ?

        W: _____, would you like a pencil?

    (2) W: _____ if I help you with the bag?

        M: Thanks _____, but I won't.

    (3) W: Could I offer you something _____?

        M: That's just _____. Thank you.

    (4) W: Would you like me to _____?

        M: If _____. But I think we'd better get someone in for a check.

    (5) W: What can I help you with?

        M: Something _____. I'm wondering if there is any chance of borrowing your _____?

        W: Sure, but mine is at home, not in the office.

        M: _____ bring it here for me tomorrow?

3. **You will hear 5 recorded questions. Listen carefully and choose the proper answer to each question. The questions will be spoken twice.**

(1) A. No, I won't. B. Yes, I do.
    C. With pleasure. D. No, I don't.

(2) A. I'd rather not. B. Thank you very much.
    C. I'm looking for a gift for my wife. D. You can do it right now.

(3) A. What is it? B. No problem.
    C. Sorry. I don't know. D. Yes, I could.

(4) A. Yes, here you are. B. Please wait a minute.
    C. Sorry, I am busy. D. Yes, certainly.

(5) A. The word means Mabel. B. Mabel is a girl's name, I think.
    C. Of Course, I'm Mabel myself. D. Sorry, I don't know, either.

Part III Passages

1. **Listen to the passage and supply the missing words. It will be read three times.**

1 People who visit the United States sometimes _____ how the states got their names. Some of the most interesting names _____ American Indian languages. For example, Illinois was named for the _____ who used to live in that part of the country. In their language, Illinois means "Brave Men." Connecticut means "At the Long River-Mouth" in the language of the Indians who used to live there.

2 Twenty-five of the states have Indian names, but other names were taken from _____. Georgia and Pennsylvania have names which were taken from the

Latin-based languages. Florida and Colorado were named for places in England. The two newest states have names which did not come from any of ＿＿＿＿＿. Hawaii got its name from a word in the Hawaiian language which means "＿＿＿＿＿." Alaska was named by the Russians, from whom Alaska was bought in 1867.

2. Listen to the passage again and answer the following questions.

(1) What does "Illinois" mean in a native language?

(2) How many states got their names from American native languages?

(3) From which language did "Georgia" take its name?

(4) What was "Florida" named for?

(5) What does "Hawaii" mean?

3. Listen to the passage and decide whether the following statements are true (T) or false (F).

___ (1) Mr. Brown and his wife decided to paint the room of the house.

___ (2) They decided to paint the house themselves because they wanted to spend less money.

___ (3) They finished the painting before evening came.

___ (4) They found everything was all right the next day.

___ (5) After painting, they felt very happy and excited. Mr. and Mrs. Brown in fact saved as much as they wished.

4. Watch the video and enjoy the movie clip.

Part IV Oral Practice

Text A

At the airport in New York, America, Hua Zhao gets off the taxi and a porter approaches to her.

Porter: Hello, Ma'am. It's a nice day, isn't it?

Zhao: Hi, sure it is. Excuse me, do you happen to know when the next plane to Shanghai takes off?

Porter: At ten to five.

Zhao: Thank you. There's about half an hour left. I wonder if you could help me to take my suitcase and box onto the plane. They're too heavy for me to carry them in.

Porter: Well, ma'am, I'm afraid I can't. But I can take your baggage to the check-in counter where you get your boarding pass and have your baggage checked in. You don't need to carry your baggage onto the airplane yourself.

Zhao: That'll be good enough.

Text B

Sohpia lost her purse when she got off the bus. Just at that time a very tall young man is coming.

Man: Excuse me, are you looking for something?

Sohpia: Yes, a purse. A purple one, with two brass rings on each side.

Man: Is this the one you were looking for?

Sohpia: Yes, thank you very much. I'm very glad to come across so kind a man like you.

Man: Would you check your purse if everything is there?

Sohpia: The money and the ring are both there. Thank you.

New Words and Expressions

approach	/əˈprəʊtʃ/	vt.	接近,动手处理
		vi.	靠近
Ma'am	/mæm/		= Madam /ˈmædəm/
suitcase	/ˈsjuːtkeɪs/	n.	手提箱,衣箱
purple	/ˈpəːpl/	a.	紫色的
brass	/brɑːs/	n.	黄铜
the check-in counter			(机场)登记处
boarding pass			(=boarding card)登机卡
come across			碰到

Proper Names

New York	/njuːˈjɔːk/	纽约
America	/əˈmerɪkə/	美国;美洲
Sohpia		苏菲亚

Task Role Play

Students act as Zhao and Porter or Sohpia and Tall man. Act out Text A or Text B.

Exercises

(1) Work in pairs and practise offering help to others.

Useful Expressions

Can I help you?	我能帮你吗？
That's all right.	好的。
You are welcome.	不用谢。
It's a pleasure.	很荣幸。

(2) Make up dialogues according to the given conditions below.

① You see an old man who doesn't look well. You want to help him.

② You see a stranger who seems to have got lost. You want to help him.

(3) Imagine you are busy writing something in the office, from outside comes a tall young lady, Xiao Xiao, a colleague. She wants to borrow a camera from you. Make up a dialogue between you and Xiao Xiao. The patterns you learned just now and the vocabulary given below may be of some help to you.

Useful Expressions

I'm wondering if...	我想是否……
a little bit	一点
shoot	拍摄

Part V Learn to Sing a Song

 1. Listen to the song "Edelweiss."

 2. Listen to the song again and fill in the missing words.

Edelweiss

Edelweiss, edelweiss
Every morning you _____ me
Small and _____
Clean and _____
You look _____ to meet me
Blossom of _____
May you bloom and _____
Bloom and grow _____
Edelweiss, edelweiss
Bless my _____ forever

3. Learn to sing the song after the singer.

UNIT FOUR

Shopping

Part 1 Phonetics

Phonetic Practice:

/tr/   /dr/   /ts/   /dz/   /tʃ/   /dʒ/

1. Listen and repeat the following words, pay attention to the colored parts.

(1) /tr/	truck	try	train	trouble	true
(2) /dr/	dry	dress	drag	drink	driver
(3) /ts/	cats	plants	sits	attracts	costs
(4) /dz/	beds	finds	reads	holds	ends
(5) /tʃ/	church	chair	catch	teacher	fetch
(6) /dʒ/	orange	fridge	John	surgeon	judge

39

2. **Listen to the poem written by Hamlin Garland "What Makes a Man?" Choose the words you hear to fill in the blanks.**

New Words

fear	/fɪə/	v.	害怕，畏惧
fight	/faɪt/	v.	打架，对抗
wolf	/wʊlf/	n.	狼
wade	/weɪd/	v.	跋涉
		n.	跋涉，可涉水而过的地方
crane	/kreɪn/	n.	鹤
palm	/pɑːm/	n.	手掌
thicken	/ˈθɪkən/	v.	使变厚，使变粗
tan	/tæn/	v.	(使)晒成棕褐色
ragged	/ˈrægɪd/	a.	破烂的，粗糙的
weary	/ˈwɪərɪ/	a.	厌倦的，令人厌烦的
swarthy	/ˈswɔːðɪ/	a.	黑黝黝的

Poem

What Makes a Man?

Hamlin Garland

Do you fear the force of the wind,
    The _____ (slash, starch) of the rain?
Go face them and fight them,
    Be _____ (savage, sedge) again.
Go hungry and cold like the wolf. Go wade like the crane.
    The palms of your hands will thicken,
    The skin of your _____ (cheeks, shake) will tan,
You'll grow ragged and weary and swarthy,
    But you'll walk like a man.

3. Read aloud the poem after the speaker sentence by sentence.

4. Practice the tongue twister sentence by sentence after the speaker. Pay attention to the sounds.

   (1) A cheeky Chimp chucked cheap chocolate chips in the cheap chocolate chip shop.

   (2) The drummers drummed and the strummers strummed.

   (3) James jostled Jean while Jean jostled Joan.

   (4) Drew dripped the drink from the dipper, but he did not drink a drop.

Part II Dialogues

Warming Up

(1) —Can I help you?

   —Yes. Do you have shoes to match this skirt?

(2) —Yes. We have quite a few different colors. Do you want high or low?

   —High. Please.

(3) —Do you like these?

   —Yes. They're very nice.

(4) —Please try them on.

   —They are a bit too large.

(5) —Which size do you want?

   —I'm not sure. In China, I take size 38.

(6) —It's 70 dollars.

   —Oh, it's so expensive. Any discount?

(7) —We can give you a 10% discount.

   — All right. I'll take it.

(8) —How about this pair?

—Let me see, hmm... I'll take this pair. How much is it?

If you are a salesman / saleswoman, you can say

(1) Can I help you?

(2) What can I do for you?

(3) What would you like to see?

(4) What do you want to buy?

(5) Would you like to choose anything now?

(6) What do you think of this?

(7) What kind would you like?

(8) Do you want to buy something here?

If you are a customer, you can say

(1) Could you please show me some...?

(2) May I look around a while first?

(3) I'd like to buy something for my friends. Could you give me some advice?

(4) I have no idea. Which one would you recommend?

(5) May I see these...?

1. **Video: Watch the video and do the activities as indicated.**

New Words and Expressions

tramp	/træmp/	n.	流浪汉
flower	/ˈflaʊə/	n.	花
sell	/sel/	v.	卖
a girl selling flower			卖花女
lose the sight of both eyes			双目失明
sympathize with sb.			同情某人
try one's best to do sth.			尽力做某事

Activities

(1) Try to use your own words to explain what you have seen in the video.

(2) What do you think of the people in the video?

(3) What do you think is the most important thing for you to learn? Why?

2. **Listen to the following short dialogues and fill in the blanks with the information you get from the tape. Each dialogue will be read twice.**

   (1) W: Mr. Woods, are you going to _____ your job on the buses?

   M: Yes, I'm going to finish _____ the week.

   (2) W: And what _____ have you got?

   M: Well, I'm going to _____.

   (3) W: Have you got _____ now?

   M: No, we live in a furnished _____.

   (4) W: Have you got _____?

   M: Yes, I've got _____, but I'm going to buy _____.

   (5) W: I'd like to have three _____ these socks. Shall I save any money if I buy a dozen?

   M: Yes. They are usually 5 dollars each, but you can have a dozen for _____ dollars.

3. **You will hear 5 recorded questions. Listen carefully and choose the proper answer to each question. The questions will be spoken twice.**

(1) A. You may get one.　　　　B. At 5:30.
　　C. Here you are.　　　　　 D. Fifty dollars.

(2) A. 168 dollars.　　　　　　B. 2 weeks.
　　C. 30 meters.　　　　　　 D. 20 years old.

(3) A. With pleasure.　　　　　B. Yes, I'd love to.
　　C. No, thanks.　　　　　　D. Yes, please.

(4) A. No, it's not mine.　　　 B. Yes. Here you are.
　　C. Sorry, I don't know him. D. Ask Lily, please.

(5) A. That's great.　　　　　　B. The book about the tea is very interesting.
　　C. How much must I pay?　 D. A glass is enough.

Part III　Passages

  1. **Listen to the passage and supply the missing words. It will be read three times.**

1　　　　Abraham Lincoln was born in a _____ family in Kentucky. As a young man, he studied law and later became a _____. He was active in politics and _____ against slavery. He became President in 1860. He worked hard for the freedom of all the people. After the American Civil War, the _____ was reunited and slaves were set free. He was elected President for the _____ time in 1864. The people loved him, but his enemies _____ him. He was _____ at a theatre in 1865. Today he is _____ one of the greatest presidents of the United States.

2. Listen to the passage again and answer the following questions.

(1) What did Lincoln study when he was young?

(2) When did he become President?

(3) He was elected president for the second time in 1864, wasn't he?

(4) Did his enemies hate him?

(5) Where was he shot?

3. Listen to the passage and decide whether the following statements are true (T) or false (F)

___ (1) Tom was a rich boy.

___ (2) Mr. Miser didn't love money.

___ (3) Tom cleaned a pair of shoes for Mr. Miser for the first time.

___ (4) The people in the street made fun of Mr. Miser because of his dirty shoe.

___ (5) Finally the rich man didn't return to clean his shoes.

4. Watch the video and enjoy the movie clip.

New Words

hairdresser	/ˈheədresə(r)/	n.	理发师
musician	/mjuːˈzɪʃən/	n.	音乐家
painter	/ˈpeɪntə/	n.	画家
model	/ˈmɒdl/	n.	模特
recognize	/ˈrekəgnaɪz/	v.	认识，认出
romantic	/rəʊˈmæntɪk/	a.	浪漫的

Part IV Oral Practice

Text A

Mr. Liu is a travel guide at a travel agency. Now he is giving shopping advice to Bill, one of his customers.

Bill: I'm thinking of buying something for my friends. Could you give me some advice?

Liu: Sure. What would you like to buy?

Bill: I'd like to buy typical Chinese products.

Liu: Then you can buy some Chinese silk products, such as embroidered handkerchiefs, tablecloth or blouses.

Bill: That's a good idea! Where can I buy them?

Liu: I suggest the First Department Store on Silver Street. It's only two blocks away from here.

Bill: Are the goods very expensive there?

Liu: No. The prices are very reasonable in the First Department Store.

Bill: Great! I'd also be interested in a bookstore.

Liu: Hum... there is a bookstore at the corner of the 8th and Silver Street—that's west of the First Department Store.

Bill: Thanks a lot.

Liu: You're welcome.

Text B

Mr. and Mrs. Brown come to the Friendship Department Store. They want to buy something for their daughter, Mary and her boy friend, David. Miss Wu, the shop assistant, serves them.

Miss Wu: What can I do for you, madam?

Mrs. Brown: Yes, may I see these ties?

Miss Wu: Certainly. Here's a nice-looking one.

Mrs. Brown: Yes, it's very attractive.

Mr. Brown: But I think it's a little too loud. David is quite conservative. (To Miss Wu) Let me see that gray and blue one.

Mrs. Brown: This one?

Mr. Brown: Yes, that one. (To Mrs. Brown) This is very nice, isn't it?

Mrs. Brown: Yes, it is. I do hope David likes it.

Miss Wu: Anything else?

Mrs. Brown: May I have a look at that hat over there?

Miss Wu: Of course. You want to buy it for yourself?

Mrs. Brown: No. I want to choose one for my daughter.

Miss Wu: Well, it is very fashionable. Would you like the red one or the green one?

Mrs. Brown: A red one, please.

Miss Wu: Here you are.

Mrs. Brown: Thanks. How much do this hat and the tie cost in all?

Miss Wu: Let me see. Two hundred and fifty—three yuan for the tie, one hundred and twenty-seven yuan for the hat. It comes to three hundred and eighty yuan.

Mr. Brown: Here is the money.

New Words and Expressions

blouse	/blaʊz/	n.	女式衬衣
bookstore	/ˈbʊkstɔː(r)/	n.	书店
embroidered	/ɪmˈbrɔɪdəd/	a.	刺绣的
handkerchief	/ˈhæŋkətʃɪːf/	n.	手帕
reasonable	/ˈriːznəbl/	a.	合理的,公道的
silver	/ˈsɪlvə/	n.	银,银器
silk	/sɪlk/	n.	丝绸
tablecloth	/ˈteɪb(ə)lklɔθ/	n.	桌布
typical	/ˈtɪpɪkəl/	a.	典型的,有代表性的
attractive	/əˈtræktɪv/	a.	引人注目的
loud	/laʊd/	a.	过分鲜艳的,俗气的
conservative	/kənˈsɜːvətɪv/	a.	保守的
fashionable	/ˈfæʃənəbl/	a.	时髦的,流行的
nice-looking	/ˈnaɪsˈlʊkɪŋ/	a.	好看的
be interested in			对……感兴趣
in all			总计

Proper Names

the Friendship Department Store   友谊商店

Task Role Play

Students act as Bill and Mr. Liu or Miss. Wu, Mrs. Brown, and Mr. Brown. Act out Text A or Text B.

Exercises

(1) Imagine you are a salesman / saleswoman and now you are doing something for a customer. Make up a dialogue between them. The patterns you learned just now and the vocabulary given below may be of some help to you.

Useful Words and Expressions

What can I do for you?	您要什么？有什么事可以为您效劳？
show sb. sth.	把……给……看
a great variety of	各种各样
What do you think of...?	你认为……怎么样？

(2) Now you and your friend have come to a shop. You want to buy something for yourself. The shop assistant serves you. Make a dialogue according to the information. The patterns you learned just now and the vocabulary given below may be of some help to you.

Useful Words and Expressions

serve	/sɜːv/	v.	服务，侍候
fit	/fit/	v.	适合
Would you like to choose anything else?			还要选点别的吗？
be made of			由……制成

Part V Learn to Sing a Song

 1. Listen to the song "My Heart Will Go On."

 2. Listen to the song again and fill in the missing words.

> Every night in my _____, I see you, I feel you
> That is how I know you go on
> Far across the _____ and spaces between us
> You have come to _____ you go on.
> Near, far, _____ you are
> I believe that the heart does go on
> Once more you open the door.
> And you're here in my heart
> And my heart will go on and on
>
> Love can _____ us one time
> And last for a lifetime

And never let go till we're gone

Love was when I loved you

One true time I _____ you.

In my life we'll _____ go on.

Near, far, wherever you are

I believe that the heart does go on

Once more you open the door

And you're here in my heart

And my heart will go on and on

You're here, there's nothing I _____

And I know that my heart will go on

We'll stay forever this way

You are safe in my heart

And my heart will go on and on

3. Learn to sing the song after the singer.

UNIT FIVE

Apologies

Part 1 Cardinals

1. **Listen to the following ten sentences twice. In each sentence there is a cardinal number. Remember the number and write it down in each of the brackets.**

    (1) (   )   (2) (   )
    (3) (   )   (4) (   )
    (5) (   )   (6) (   )
    (7) (   )   (8) (   )
    (9) (   )   (10) (   )

New Words and Expressions

earn	/ɜːn/	v.	赚,挣得,获得
cost	/kɔst/	v.	(使)花费(金钱,时间,劳力等)

2. There are ten numbers in the following sentences. Each one will be read twice. Listen carefully and write them down.

(1) (　　　　　)　　　　(2) (　　　　　)
(3) (　　　　　)　　　　(4) (　　　　　)
(5) (　　　　　)　　　　(6) (　　　　　)
(7) (　　　　　)　　　　(8) (　　　　　)
(9) (　　　　　)　　　　(10) (　　　　　)

New Words and Expressions

QQ	/ˈkjuːkjuː/	n.	一种即时互动通信软件
password	/ˈpɑːswɜːd/	n.	密码,口令
operator	/ˈɔpəreɪtə/	n.	(电话)接线员
area code			电话地区号
short message	/ʃɔːtˈmesɪdʒ/		短消息
rent	/rent/	v.	租,租借

3. Listen to the poem written by an unknown writer. Choose the words you hear to fill in the blanks.

New Words and Expressions

anon. = anonymous	/əˈnɒnɪməs/	a.	作者不详的，无名的，佚名的
comely	/ˈkʌmlɪ/	a.	清秀的，标致的
grace	/ɡreɪs/	n.	优美，雅致，优雅
pleasing	/ˈpliːzɪŋ/	a.	令人高兴的，愉快的，合意的
constant	/ˈkɒnstənt/	a.	不变的，持续的，坚决的

Poem

Anon

Love me not for _____ (comely, copy) grace,

Nor for my pleasing eye or face,

Nor for any _____ (outward, outworld) part,

No, nor for my constant _____ (hot, heart), —

For those may fail, or turn to ill,

So you and I shall _____ (fall, fail) apart:

Keep therefore a true woman's eye,
And love me still, but know not why—
So have you the _____ (some, same) reason still
To love me forever!

4. Read aloud the poem after the speaker sentence by sentence.

5. Practice the tongue twister sentence by sentence after the speaker. Pay attention to the sounds.

A big black bear bit the back of a big black pig
Then a big black bug bit the back of the big black bear
And then the big black bug bit the big black bear
The big black pig bit back the big black bear

Part II   Dialogues

Warming Up

Expressions commonly used in an apology

(1) Excuse me for my smoking here.

(2) Please forgive me. I really didn't mean that.

(3) I'm sorry. I didn't mean to hurt your feelings.

(4) I apologize for what I said just now.

(5) I do beg your pardon for the trouble.

(6) Please excuse me coming late.

(7) Please forgive my for having lost your letter.

(8) I'm afraid I've brought you too much trouble.

Expressions used in responding to an apology

(1) Don't think any more about it.

(2) It doesn't matter at all.

(3) It's just too bad.

(4) It's not your fault.

(5) Never mind. It doesn't really matter.

(6) Please don't give it another thought.

(7) Please think nothing of it.

(8) There's no reason to apologize.

Expressions used in leaving somebody politely for a short time

(1) Excuse me.

(2) Excuse me. I'll be back in a minute.

(3) I'm afraid I must leave you for a short while.

(4) I wonder if you'd excuse me for a moment.

(5) Would you excuse me for a moment, please?

1. **Video: Watch the video and do the activities as indicated.**

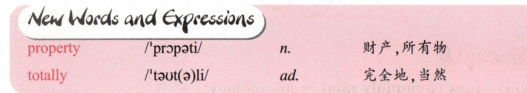

| property | /ˈprɔpəti/ | n. | 财产,所有物 |
| totally | /ˈtəut(ə)li/ | ad. | 完全地,当然 |

Activities

(1) Try to use your own words to explain what you have seen in the video.

(2) What do you want to make the room?

(3) What do you think is the most important thing for you to learn? Why?

2. **Listen to the following short dialogues and fill in the blanks with the information you get from the tape. Each dialogue will be read twice.**

   (1) M: Be _____.

   W: Why? What's _____?

   M: You're _____ on my foot.

   W: Oh, sorry.

   (2) W: Tyler, the kitchen is _____ dirty!

   M: Yeah, I know.

   W: So do the dishes now! And clean the floor!

   M: Why _____ you do it?

   W: I do it _____ now it's your turn.

   M: Oh, okay. You're right. It's _____.

   (3) M: Is there _____ pizza?

   W: No. We don't have _____, sorry.

   M: Well, are there _____ apples?

   W: Er, yes, there's _____ in the kitchen. Help yourself.

   (4) M: Hi, Linda, _____ the ice cream?

   W: It's in the refrigerator.

   M: No, it's not. It's _____.

   W: Oh, sorry. It's _____ next to the milk.

   M: Great! Thank you.

   (5) M: Waitress, what happened to _____? We've waited for 10 minutes.

   W: I'm sorry, sir. I'll see the _____ for you.

   M: Well, please hurry up. We can't wait _____.

   W: I'll be with you _____.

   W: I'm _____ to have kept you waiting. Your order is coming, sir.

Unit Five

59

M: All right. Thank you.

W: Please _____ your drinks.

3. **You will hear 5 recorded questions. Listen carefully and choose the proper answer to each question. The questions will be spoken twice.**

(1) A. You're right, sir. B. Let me tell you.

　　C. Wang Ling speaking. D. Thank you very much.

(2) A. Sorry, Mr. Wang is not in at the moment.

　　B. Mr. Wang is our boss.

　　C. Xiao Li speaking.

　　D. Sorry, sir. I can't tell you.

(3) A. Sorry, sir. What's the problem? B. May I speak to Mr. Wang, please?

　　C. No problem. D. My car broke down this morning.

(4) A. That's all for now. B. I'll wait for you.

　　C. My wife left me this morning. D. I can't see you.

(5) A. Today is Monday. B. Tomorrow from 8 a.m. to 2 p.m.

　　C. I can't go to work today. D. I want to see Mr. Wang.

Part III Passages

1. Listen to the passage and supply the missing words. It will be read three times.

Hearts Like Doors

1   Hearts like doors will open with ease,
2   To _____ ,
3   And don't forget that two of these
4   Are "_____" and "_____
     _____."
5   Sometimes _____ we make with our angry words are the worst kind. Yes, we should always apologize and tell others _____ _____ when we hurt them. But our families and friends _____ if we simply learned to control our anger in the first place. If so, think how much _____ our life would be.

2. Listen to the passage again and answer the following questions.

(1) Do you think the two keys are unimportant?

(2) Can angry words hurt others?

(3) What should we do if we hurt somebody else?

(4) Is it better to control our anger in the first place?

(5) What would our life be if we don't hurt others?

3. Listen to the passage and decide whether the following statements are true (T) or false (F).

New Words and Expressions

inquiry	/ɪnˈkwaɪərɪ/	n.	调查
recommendation	/ˌrekəmenˈdeɪʃən/	n.	推荐,介绍(信)
opportunity	/ˌɔpəˈtjuːnətɪ/	n.	机会
activity	/ækˈtɪvɪtɪ/	n.	行动,活动
congressman	/ˈkɔŋgresmən/	n.	国会议员
signature	/ˈsɪgnɪtʃə/	n.	签名
register	/ˈredʒɪstə/	v.	登记,注册

___ (1) The first National Sorry Day was in 1998.

___ (2) The report *Bringing Them Home* was written in 1997.

___ (3) The report recommended that a National Sorry Day be set up.

___ (4) A lot of activities took place in America.

___ (5) People can sign their names online.

4. Watch the video and enjoy the movie clip.

New Words and Expressions

(not) in the mood			(没)有心情
stuff	/stʌf/	n.	原料,材料
jerk	/dʒɜːk/	n.	性情古怪的人
out of line			不成直线,不协调
fur	/fəː/	n.	毛皮
perspective	/pəˈspektiv/	n.	透视图,远景,观察

Part IV Oral Practice

Text A

Helen: Hello, John. You didn't come to the meeting yesterday.

John: Hello, Helen. I'm awfully sorry about all that.

Helen: Then, what is your excuse?

John: I wanted to come to the meeting but, in fact, my father was dangerously ill at that time.

Helen: Oh, is that so? I can understand.

John: Thank you for your kindness. I feel so sorry about that.

Helen: OK. It's nothing. Don't think any more about it.

Text B

Receptionist: Good morning. Fine Photocopy Company. Can I help you?

Mr. Liu: Good morning. I want to complain.

Receptionist: Oh dear. What seems to be the problem?

Mr. Liu: Just recently we bought one of your photocopiers and it's been a

	complete disaster. It breaks down every day and we've even lost a few clients.
Receptionist:	Can you be a bit more specific, please?
Mr. Liu:	Of course I can. Just this morning we called for a technician. Not only did she arrive late, but she said she could only stay for ten minutes as she had to be somewhere else. And before I could say anything she was gone. Now what kind of service do you call that?
Receptionist:	I'm awfully sorry, sir. Do you have the name of the technician who we sent?
Mr. Liu:	No, I do not, but Goody Photocopy Company can't have that many technicians, can it?
Receptionist:	I'm sorry, sir, but did you say Goody Photocopy Company?
Mr. Liu:	Yes I did. What's the problem?
Receptionist:	I'm sorry, sir, but we are the Fine Photocopy Company. I think you've made a mistake.
Mr. Liu:	Oh, so I have. Sorry about that. Do you happen to have the number for Goody Photocopy Company?
Receptionist:	No, I'm very sorry sir. I don't. Have a nice day, sir.
Mr. Liu:	Oh, yes, bye and, er, sorry.

New Words and Expressions

receptionist	/rɪˈsepʃənɪst/	n.	招待员,接话员
complain	/kəmˈpleɪn/	v.	抱怨,控诉
photocopier	/ˈfəʊtəʊkɒpɪə(r)/	n.	复印机
complete	/kəmˈpliːt/	a.	全部的,完全的
disaster	/dɪˈzɑːstə/	n.	灾难
client	/ˈklaɪənt/	n.	顾客,客户
specific	/spɪˈsɪfɪk/	a.	明确的
technician	/tekˈnɪʃ(ə)n/	n.	技术员

Task Role Play

Students act as Helen and John, or Receptionist and Mr. Liu. Act out Text A or Text B.

Exercises

(1) Imagine you are a student and you are late for English class. Make up a dialogue between your English teacher and you. The patterns you learned just now may be of some help to you.

(2) Imagine you are a receptionist of Lifan company. A customer is complaining about the new car he just bought.　Please make up a dialogue according to the information given below.

① the car

   Lifan 520.

② time (when?)

   2002-01-05.

③ where

   Shangqiao, Chongqing.

④ problem

   The front glass is broken.

⑤ demand

   Repair it today.

⑥ reply

   Repair it tomorrow.

Part V Learn to Sing a Song

 1. Listen to the song "Black and Blue."

 2. Listen to the song again and fill in the missing words.

> **Black and Blue**
>
> Even a lover makes a mistake sometimes,
>
> _____ any other fall out and lose his mind.
>
> And I'm sorry for the things I did.
>
> For your tear drops over words I say.
>
> _____ happens I know that I was wrong.
>
> Oh, yeah,
>
> Can you believe me maybe your faith is gone.
>
> _____ I love you and I always will
>
> So I wonder if you want me still
>
> Can you _____ me?
>
> Open your heart once again.
>
> Oh, yeah,
>
> It is true, I mean it.
>
> From the bottom of my heart,
>
> Yes it's true, without you I would fall apart.
>
> I'd do everything to _____ to you.
>
> So please understand.

3. Learn to sing the song after the singer.

UNIT SIX

Going to a Party

Part 1   Ordinals

1. **Listen to the following ten sentences twice. In each sentence there is an ordinal number. Remember the number and write it down in each of the brackets.**

   (1) (   )   (2) (   )
   (3) (   )   (4) (   )
   (5) (   )   (6) (   )
   (7) (   )   (8) (   )
   (9) (   )   (10) (   )

2. Listen to the following ten sentences. Each one will be read twice. Listen carefully and write them down.

(1)

(2)

(3)

(4)

(5)

(6)

(7)

(8)

(9)

(10)

3. Listen to the poem written by Emily Dickinson "Little Stone." Choose the words you hear to fill in the blanks.

New Words

ramble	/ˈræmbl/	v.	漫游,漫步
exigency	/ˈeksɪdʒənsɪ/	n.	苛求;紧急,紧急事件
independent	/ˌɪndɪˈpendənt/	a.	独立自主的,不受约束的
glow	/gləu/	v.	发光;发热
decree	/dɪˈkriː/	n.	法令,教令;天命;判决

Poem

Little Stone

Emily Dickinson

How happy is the little stone

That rambles in _____ (road, load) alone,

And doesn't care about _____ (Korea, careers)

And Exigencies never fears

Whose _____ (goat, coat) of elemental Brown

A passing _____ (universe, universal) put on,

And independent as the Sun

Associates or glows alone,

Fulfilling _____ (absolute, almost) Decree

In casual _____ (simple, simplicity)

4. Read aloud the poem sentence by sentence after the speaker.

5. Practice the tongue twister sentence by sentence after the speaker. Pay attention to the sounds.

So she bought a bit of butter,

better than her bitter butter,

and she baked it in her batter,

and the batter was not bitter.

So it was better Betty Botter,

bought a bit of better butter.

Part II Dialogues

Warming Up

Expressions used in asking somebody to a party

(1) Would you like to go to a party tonight?

(2) Would 8:00 be OK?

(3) Are you going to have a party?

(4) Can you come to my party?

(5) I love meeting new people and making new friends.

(6) I never know what to say to people I don't know.

(7) I always worry about what clothes to wear.

Responses to going to a party

(1) That sounds like a good idea.

(2) That's fine. I'm looking forward to it.

(3) I don't care for parties. They're too noisy.

(4) Sure, I'd love to.

(5) Sorry, I can't.

(6) I have to go to a piano lesson.

1. **Video:** Watch the video and do the activities as indicated.

New Words and Expressions

How'd it go? = How was it?		怎么样啦?
So now I'm taking a flight on Monday instead.		所以我现在准备改搭星期一的班机走。
Hear, hear!		说吧,让我们听一听!(这种表达含有赞同的意思。)
going-away present		离别礼物
engrave	/ɪnˈgreɪv/ v.	雕刻;使铭记
We thought alike = We thought the same thought / We shared the same idea		

Activities

(1) Try to use your own words to explain what you have seen in the video.

(2) What do you think of going-away present?

(3) What do you think is the most important thing for you to learn? Why?

2. Listen to the following short dialogues and fill in the blanks with the information you get from the tape. Each dialogue will be read twice.

(1) W: Are you going to the Johnson's party tomorrow night?

M: I don't think so. I _____ and my wife will be out of town.

(2) M: We're having _____ for Alice this evening. Would you like to join us?

W: I'd love to, but I'm going to see a play with Sally.

(3) M: _____ Andrew and Mary now?

W: That sounds like a good idea. It's been a long time since we've had any visitors.

(4) M: What was the party like?

W: _____ I don't know when I've enjoyed myself so much.

(5) M: Did you _____ at Sally's party last night?

W: We didn't get there.

3. You will hear 5 short dialogues twice. Listen carefully and choose the proper answer to each question.

(1) A. His secretary. B. His boss.

C. His partner. D. His employee.

(2) A. In a car. B. In an office.

C. In a restaurant. D. In a supermarket.

(3) A. She agreed with the man. B. She seldom takes a walk.

C. She agrees with the man. D. She doesn't agree with the man.

(4) A. He will lend his car to the woman.

B. He suggested that the woman should repair her car.

C. He won't lend his car to the woman.

D. His car is of high quality.

(5) A. There is a downpour outside.

B. It is sunny outside.

C. It is raining outside, but it will stop soon.

D. It seems that it is going to rain.

Part III Passages

1. Listen to the passage and supply the missing words. It will be read three times.

1   For the purpose of public _____, each state in the United States is divided into school districts, areas which usually include a city or a county. Each school district is run by a group of elected officials called the school _____.

2   The money to operate public schools is raised through property taxes collected by the county. Sometimes additional money may come from a state's general fund, from a state lottery, or from the federal government. School boards must then decide how to spend the money they _____.

3   Many agencies influence the decisions of the school board. The PTA (Parents' and Teachers' Association) and other citizen _____ give the board their opinions. Labor unions, church groups and government agencies are very influential. The United States Supreme Court _____ that local schools are run within the guidelines of the United States Constitution.

2. Listen to the passage again and answer the following questions.

(1) Who runs school districts in the United States?

(2) How do people collect money in order to operate public schools?

(3) According to the passage, who has the power to decide the spending of schools' money?

(4) Which agencies influence the decisions of the school board?

(5) What role does the United States Supreme Court play in the management of local schools?

3. Listen to the passage and decide whether the following statements are true (T) or false (F).

___ (1) School districts include a city or a country.

___ (2) Public schools are only supported by property taxes in the United States.

___ (3) The federal government never gives money to public schools.

___ (4) Church groups also influence the decisions of the school board.

___ (5) Any citizen can give their opinions to the school board.

4. Watch the video and enjoy the movie clip.

New Words

judge	/dʒʌdʒ/	n.	法官,裁判员,鉴赏家
wedding	/ˈwedɪŋ/	n.	婚礼,婚宴,结婚典礼
ceremony	/ˈserɪmənɪ/	n.	典礼,仪式,礼节
holy	/ˈhəʊlɪ/	a.	神圣的,圣洁的
matrimony	/ˈmætrɪmənɪ/	n.	结婚
legally	/ˈliːgəlɪ/	a.	法律上,合法地
lawful	/ˈlɔːfəl/	a.	法律许可的,守法的

vest	/vest/	n.	背心
		v.	使穿衣服,授予
pronounce	/prəˈnaʊns/	v.	发音,宣告,断言
bride	/braɪd/	n.	新娘

Part IV Oral Practice

Text A

(Dan calls Kay.)

Dan: Hello, Kay. It's Dan. I just received the invitation to your party.

Kay: Can you make it?

Dan: Well, let's see. It's next Friday night, 7:30 pm, at 166 Wetland Road. Right?

Kay: That's right. I hope you can come?

Dan: It would be my pleasure. Can I bring anything?

Kay: Just yourself.

Dan: Ok. I'll be there with bells on. I'm looking forward to it. Thanks.

Kay: Bye.

Dan: See you then.

Text B

(Dan and the other guests at the party.)

Bill: Hi! How are you?

Dan: Fine. How about you?

Bill: Super! Let me introduce you to my niece, Claire. Claire, this is Dan—he works with me at the office.

Claire: Hello, Dan.

Bill: Dan, this is my brother John's daughter, Claire.

Dan: Pleased to meet you. I didn't know John had a daughter. Where's he been hiding you?

Bill: She's been living out East with his wife's sister. She just moved back.

Dan: What part of the East, Claire?

Claire: Boston, near the harbor.

Dan: It must be quite a change—coming back here?

Claire: It is, but I'm glad to be back and see all my friends.

Bill: Hey, Dan. Do you still play golf?

Dan: Not as much as I would like.

Bill: Claire plays. Maybe we could all play sometime soon?

Dan: That sounds great. How about tomorrow morning?

B.&C.: Sure, say 7:00, out at Harrison Park?

Dan: Great, 7 a.m. at Harrison. I look forward to it.

Kay: (rejoining the group) I see you've met Elizabeth.

Dan: Elizabeth? (to Claire) I thought your name was Claire?

Claire: It is. My aunt just calls me by Elizabeth.

Dan: Well, I've not only met Elizabeth, but the three of us are off to the greens in the morning.

Kay: She'll probably whip both of you! Ha Ha.

Bill: Dan, could you pass me that newspaper? Let's see what the weather's supposed to be.

Dan: Sure, here you go.

Bill: Thanks.

Claire: How often do you play, Dan?

Dan: Well, this year I've only played twice. How about you?

Claire: I was playing weekly in Boston—with my aunt, but since I came home I haven't played once.

Bill: The report is a humdinger. I guess the leftovers from hurricane Opal are gone.

Dan: So are you saying it is supposed to be nice tomorrow?
Bill: I am sure. It says it will be sunny and dry—perfect weather.
Kay: Enough about golf. How's your dancing? Hey, Peter. Would you turn up the stereo? We've got a party going on!

New Words and Expressions

super	/ˈsjuːpə/	a.	极好的
niece	/niːs/	n.	侄女
hide	/haɪd/	v.	隐藏,躲藏
harbor	/ˈhɑːbə/	n.	港口
golf	/gɔlf/	n.	高尔夫(球)
say	/seɪ/	v.	假设
rejoin	/ˌriːˈdʒɔɪn/	v.	再次加入
whip	/(h)wɪp/	v.	打败,赢,胜过
suppose	/səˈpəuz/	v.	应该,假设
humdinger	/ˈhʌmdɪŋgə(r)/	n.	[美俚] 极出色的人(或事物)
leftover	/ˈleft‚ouvə/	n.	剩余物
hurricane	/ˈhʌrɪkən, -kɪn/	n.	飓风,暴风,台风
perfect	/ˈpəːfɪkt/	a.	极好的
stereo	/ˈstɪərɪəu/	n.	立体声电唱机

Proper Names

Dan	/dæn/	丹(男子名,Daniel 的昵称)
Kay	/keɪ/	凯(女子名)
Wetland Road		维特兰路
Claire	/klɛə/	克莱尔(女子名)
John	/dʒɔn/	约翰
Boston	/ˈbɔstən/	波士顿(美国马萨诸塞州首府)
Harrison Park		哈理森公园

(the) East		（美国）东部
Elizabeth	/ɪˈlɪzəbəθ/	伊丽莎白
Opal	/ˈəupəl/	奥珀尔（女子名）
Peter	/ˈpiːtə/	彼得（男子名）

Task Role Play

Students act as Dan and Kay or Bill, Claire, and Peter. Act out Text A or Text B.

Exercises

(1) You are invited to a Halloween party by the International Students' Organization. You want to go, but you lost the invitation with the information on it. You look up the International Students' Organization's telephone number and call for the information. Make up a dialogue according to the information above.

Useful Expressions

Halloween	/ˈhæləuˈiːn/	n.	万圣节前夕，诸圣日前夕
host	/həust/	n.	主人
		v.	当主人招待
look forward to (doing) sth.			期望，期待，盼望（做）某事
by the way			顺便

(2) Imagine you are going to attend your friend's birthday party. Before that, you want to confirm some information about the birthday party. Please make up a dialogue according to the information given below.

① when

　　5 p.m., this weekend

② where

　　at my home

③ Who are invited?

　　Some friends and...

④ anything else

　　refreshment, dancing...

Part V　Learn to Sing a Song

　1. Listen to the song "Ding Dong Bell."

　2. Listen to the song again and fill in the missing words.

Going to a Party

Billy Burnette

Being with you, today

Getting to _____ you in each and every way

Night times have: what can I say

Get on down and _____ me all the way

I feel a _____ lot better

I feel so _____, just a feeling this way

I'd like to _____ you and love you forever

So get on down and love me all the way

Some will; some won't

Some do; some don't

Get on down and love me all the way

3. Learn to sing the song after the singer.

UNIT SEVEN

Seeing the Doctor

Part 1   Teen's and Ten's

1. **Listen to the following ten sentences twice. In each sentence there is a number. Remember the number and write it down in each of the brackets.**

   (1) (   )   (2) (   )
   (3) (   )   (4) (   )
   (5) (   )   (6) (   )
   (7) (   )   (8) (   )
   (9) (   )   (10) (   )

80

2. **Listen to the following ten sentences. Each one will be read twice. Listen carefully and write them down.**

   (1) _____ .
   (2) _____ .
   (3) _____ .
   (4) _____ .
   (5) _____ .
   (6) _____ .
   (7) _____ .
   (8) _____ .
   (9) _____ .
   (10) _____ .

3. **Listen to the poem "The Music Within" written by Lester Garrett. Choose the words you hear to fill in the blanks.**

New Words

radiance	/ˈreɪdɪəns/	n.	光辉
surge	/sɜːdʒ/	n.	汹涌
bountiful	/ˈbaʊntɪfʊl/	a.	慷慨的
awareness	/əˈwɛənɪs/	n.	意识

Poem

The Music Within

By Lester Garrett

Life... what is it?

See it in the colors of _____.

A gentle _____ in winter,

A sudden _____ in spring.

The _____ of a summer day.

Behold it in the _____.

Of the young and the old.

Know of it in a _____.

The _____ that are bountiful.

What is life?

It is joy, _____.

And the music within.

4. Read aloud the poem after the speaker sentence by sentence.

5. Practice the tongue twister sentence by sentence after the speaker. Pay attention to the sounds.

All I want is a proper cup of coffee made in a proper copper coffee pot.

You can believe it or not,

But I just want a cup of coffee in a proper coffee pot.

Tin coffee pots or iron coffee pots are of no use to me.

If I can't have a proper cup of coffee in a proper copper coffee pot,

I'll have a cup of tea.

Part II Dialogues

Warming Up

Sentences commonly used by patients

(1) Does this medicine have any side effects?

(2) What should I do if I have another attack?

(3) Will surgery be necessary?

(4) What kind of food should I eat?

(5) Should I have a special diet?

(6) Please show me the doctor's prescription.

(7) I hate injections.

(8) Can I take the medicine orally?

Sentences commonly used by medical personnel

(1) You need a thorough examination.

(2) Have you been with anyone who has a cold?

(3) Is there any history of heart disease in your family?

(4) Have you noticed any of these symptoms recently?

(5) Point with your finger where it hurts the most.

(6) Let me make an appointment for you. Here is the card. Please try to be punctual.

(7) I'd like you to have an X-ray and after you have it, come back to me.

(8) Please take your temperature.

1. **Video: Watch the video and do the activities as indicated.**

New Words and Expressions

jail	/dʒeɪl/	n.	监狱
scream	/skriːm/	v.	尖叫,吼叫
guard	/gɑːd/	n.	哨兵,门卫
escape	/ɪsˈkeɪp/	v.	逃跑,逃避
prison	/ˈprɪzn/	v.	监禁;紧紧抱住

Activities

(1) Try to use your own words to explain what you have seen in the video.

(2) What do you think of your strange character?

(3) What do you think is the most important thing for you to learn? Why?

2. **Listen to the following short dialogues and fill in the blanks with the information you get from the tape. Each dialogue will be read twice.**

   Doctor: I see you _____ last July. Has anything else troubled you?

   Patient: I've kept _____ in my ears and giddiness.

   Doctor: Anything else?

   Patient: Yes. I am _____ .

   Doctor: _____ ?

   Patient: Say, Six months.

   Doctor: Since your _____ with iron?

   Patient: Yes. I keep _____ .

   Doctor: Do you _____ ?

   Patient: Yes. First thing in the morning, _____ .

   Doctor: You say you are breathless?

   Patient: Yes. _____ .

3. **You will hear 5 recorded questions. Listen carefully and choose the proper answer to each question. The questions will be spoken twice.**

   (1) A. It never hurts.   B. It started hurting last Sunday.
       C. She'll have it filled.   D. It had never been filled.

   (2) A. Her son was ill.   B. She was ill.
       C. She was fired.   D. She had to give up her job.

   (3) A. She returned to work last week.
       B. She has had an operation.
       C. She is still being treated in the hospital.
       D. She'll rest at home for another two weeks.

(4) A. Because it's really effective. B. Because it only works temporarily.

C. Because it doesn't work. D. Because it has harmful side effects.

(5) A. He fell down the stairs.

B. He was hurt while playing volleyball.

C. His car was hit by another car.

D. He was hit by a car when crossing the street.

Part III Passages

1. Listen to the passage and supply the missing words. It will be read three times.

1 When William Smith was twenty, he took part in a lot of sports games, and he was thin and strong. But after thirty years, he began to get fat and slow. He can't _____ as well as before, and his heart beat _____ from time to time.

2 He didn't pay any attention to it for a long time, but at last he became _____ and went to see a doctor, and soon the doctor sent him to the hospital. A very young intern (实习医师) _____ him and said: "I'm very sorry, sir. I don't want to lie. I must tell you the truth. Believe me you are very ill and it isn't _____ for you to live longer. Would you like to see anybody or have anybody come and see you before you die?"

3 William thought for a moment and answered: "I'd like to have another doctor come and see me."

2. **Listen to the passage again and answer the following questions.**

   (1) How old was William Smith when he began to get fat and slow?

   (2) What was the trouble with William?

   (3) What did William Smith do about the trouble?

   (4) Who thought William was going to die soon?

   (5) Do you think William trusted the young doctor? Why or why not?

3. **Listen to another passage and decide whether the following statements are true (T) or false (F).**

   ___ (1) According to the author, the reason why people should take care of health is that the cost of medical care is so high.

   ___ (2) To keep fit, you need enough good food, enough sleep and little relax.

   ___ (3) Becoming ill will waste you much time and money.

   ___ (4) Like any machine, people need proper care.

   ___ (5) According to the passage, it is not very important to have regular medical check-ups.

4. **Watch the video and enjoy the movie clip.**

New Words

fingerprint	/ˈfɪŋgəprɪnt/	n.	指纹,手印
		v.	采指纹
forgive	/fəˈgɪv/	v.	原谅,饶恕
mask	/mɑːsk/	n.	面具
		v.	戴面具,掩饰
put sb. through			使某人经受,遭受
in this mess			陷于窘境;一团乱

Part IV Oral Practice

Text A

The following is a story happening on the phone between a patient and a nurse.

Patient: Hello, is that Dr. Michael Yang's office?

Nurse: Yes, can I help you?

Patient: I wonder if Dr. Yang will be free to make an appointment with me?

Nurse: Yes, of course. What's the trouble, sir?

Patient: I have a terrible stomachache. I'd like to see him this morning.

Nurse: I'm afraid Dr. Yang is busy today. How about the day after tomorrow?

Patient: No, that'll be too late. Can't he see me this afternoon?

Nurse: I'm afraid he can't. Can't you wait for two days?

Patient: Sorry, my stomach can't wait.

Text B

Zhao has been sick in bed for three days now with a terrible headache and a bad stomachache and now he is sure he also has a fever. He calls his friend Wu.

Wu: Hello, who is calling, please?

Zhao: Wu? Is that you?

Wu: Yes. Who is that?

Zhao: This is Zhao speaking.

Wu: Hi. How are you?

Zhao: (cough)

Wu: What's the matter with you?

Zhao: As a matter of fact, I'm rather sick. That's why I called you. I've had a bad stomachache and a terrible headache for three days now, and I think I need a doctor.

Wu: Do you have any temperature?

Zhao: I think so. I feel I'm burning up. I need a doctor, but I can't go to the clinic by myself.

Wu: Don't worry. Take out your medical insurance and your personal health record. I'll drive over and pick you up.

Zhao: Thanks a lot. Bye.

New Words and Expressions

intern	/ɪnˈtɜːn/	n.	实习医师
		v.	作实习医师
stomachache	/ˈstʌməkeɪk/	n.	胃痛,肚子痛
temperature	/ˈtemprətʃə(r)/	n.	温度
fever	/ˈfiːvə/	n.	发烧,发热
		v.	(使)发烧
clinic	/ˈklɪnɪk/	n.	诊所,门诊部,临床
burn up			燃烧起来
as a matter of fact			事实上

medical insurance	医疗保险
health record	健康记录

Task Role Play

Students act as patient and doctor or nurse. Act out Text A or Text B.

Exercises

(1) Imagine you are a patient who has a terrible toothache because of eating too much candy, your classmate suggests that you go to see a dentist. Make up a dialogue between you and your classmate. The patterns you learned just now and the vocabulary given below may be of some help to you.

Useful Words and Expressions

decay	/dɪˈkeɪ/	v. & n.	腐朽,腐烂;衰减
dentist	/ˈdentɪst/	n.	牙科医生
tartar	/ˈtɑːtə/	n.	酒石;[医]牙垢
gum	/gʌm/	n.	牙龈;橡胶;口香糖
scratch	/skrætʃ/	n.	抓痕;擦伤
		v.	擦,刮
decayed tooth			虫牙,龋齿
fill a tooth			补牙
pain-killer			止痛药
pull out a tooth			拔牙
remove the tartar from your teeth			去除牙石

(2) Suppose you are a patient, you go to see the doctor and then your friend drives you to the drugstore. Please make up a dialogue according to the information given below and act it out.

Characters:

Patient—Wang

Doctor—Bell
A friend of Patient—Susan
Druggist—Welsh

Scene one:

Place: In the hospital

Situation: Wang has the flu, doctor Bell examines him and suggests that he go home and rest for a couple of days.

Scene two:

Place: In the drugstore

Situation: Susan drops Wang off at the drugstore to have the prescriptions filled. Wang takes the medicine and asks druggist Welsh carefully about usage of the medicine.

Useful Expressions

examine	/ɪgˈzæmɪn/	v.	检查,调查,考试
headache	/ˈhedeɪk/	n.	头痛,令人头痛之事
cough	/kɔːf/	n.	咳嗽
		v.	咳嗽
prescribe	/prɪsˈkraɪb/	v.	指示,规定,处(方),开(药)
prescription	/prɪˈskrɪpʃən/	n.	指示,命令,处方,药方
druggist	/ˈdrʌgɪst/	n.	药剂师,药材商
tablespoonful	/ˈteɪb(ə)lspuːnfʊl/	n.	一大汤匙的量
sore throat			喉咙痛
have the prescriptions filled			(按处方)配药;抓药

Part V Learn to Sing a Song

 1. Listen to the song "Over the Rainbow."

2. Listen to the song again and fill in the missing words.

Over the Rainbow

Somewhere over the _____ way up high

There's a land that I _____ once in a lullaby

Somewhere over the rainbow _____

And the dreams that you _____ really do come true

Someday I'll wish upon a star

And _____ where the clouds are far behind me

Where troubles melt like _____ away among the chimney tops

That's where you'll find me

Somewhere over the rainbow skies are blue

And the dreams that you dare to dream really do _____

If happy little bluebirds fly _____ the rainbow

Why or why can't I?

3. Learn to sing the song after the singer.

UNIT EIGHT

A Job Interview

Part 1   General Questions and Special Questions

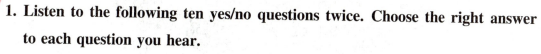

🎧 **1. Listen to the following ten yes/no questions twice. Choose the right answer to each question you hear.**

(1) A. Yes, she did.   B. Yes, she was.   C. Yes, she is.

(2) A. No, I am not.   B. No, I wasn't.   C. No, I didn't.

(3) A. No, he didn't.   B. No, he wasn't.   C. No, he doesn't.

(4) A. Yes, she has.   B. Yes, she was.   C. Yes, she is.

(5) A. No, I won't.   B. No, she won't.   C. No, she doesn't.

(6) A. Yes, I can't.   B. No, I couldn't.   C. No, I can't.

(7) A. Yes, she did.   B. Yes, she does.   C. Yes, she is.

(8) A. Yes, she did. B. Yes, she was. C. Yes, she will.
(9) A. Yes, she did. B. Yes, she was. C. Yes, she is.
(10) A. Yes, she did. B. Yes, she was. C. Yes, she is.

2. There are five wh-questions twice. Listen carefully and choose the correct answer.

(1) A. 3. B. Chinese, English. C. Computer.
(2) A. In the afternoon. B. Over there. C. Six months.
(3) A. Mary. B. In the school. C. 2 desks.
(4) A. It look like a ball. B. It is a ball. C. It looks like a ball.
(5) A. Very clearly. B. Last year. C. In the church.

3. Listen to the poem quoted from The Bible. Choose the words you hear to fill in the blanks.

New Words

envy	/ˈenvɪ/	n.	嫉妒,羡慕
self-seeking	/ˌselfˈsiːkɪŋ/	a.	追求私利的
wrong	/rɔŋ/	n.	坏事,恶行
persevere	/ˌpɜːsɪˈvɪə/	v.	坚持不懈;坚韧

Poem

LOVE

Love is _____ (patient, patina), love is kind. It does not envy, it does not _____ (poster, boast), it is not proud.

It is not _____ (proud, rude), it is not self-seeking, it is not easily angered, it keeps no _____ (recruit, record) of wrongs.

Love does not _____ (delete, delight) in evil but _____ (rejoices, rejoins) with the truth.

It always protects, always _____ (trusts, rusts), always hopes, always perseveres.

Love never _____ (faints, fails).

4. Read aloud the poem after the speaker sentence by sentence.

5. Practice the tongue twister sentence by sentence after the speaker.
   Pay attention to the sounds.

   If you understand, say "understand."

   If you don't understand, say "don't understand."

   But if you understand and say "don't understand."

   How do I understand that you understand? Understand!

Part II Dialogues

Warming Up

Questions you may be asked by an interviewer

(1) Would you like to introduce yourself first?

(2) How well did you do in school?

(3) What are your strong points and weak points?

(4) How would your friends describe you?

(5) What are your hobbies?

(6) What do you know about our company?

(7) Why do you want to work for this company?

(8) What salary do you expect?

Responses you may use in the interview

(1) I think this job is a challenge for me.

(2) I don't think there is any problem for me to work on a computer.

(3) I don't have any experience, but I can learn quickly and I'll try my best.

(4) I visited your website and had a careful study of your career programs for employees. I think they are quite attractive.

(5) My friends would say I am easy to get along with and hard-working.

(6) I am a self-motivated hard worker. As to my weakness, I guess that I don't have strong analytic skills.

(7) Based on my skills and experience, I am looking for 1000 *yuan* per month.

(8) If you give me the opportunity, I think I can meet your requirements.

Questions you may want to ask the interviewer

(1) How many hours would I work?

(2) May I ask about the pay?

(3) Would I have to work overtime very often?

(4) Would there be any opportunities to work abroad in the future?

(5) May I ask how much the bonuses are?

(6) How about the vacations and sick leave?

1. Video: Watch the video and do the activities as indicated.

New Words and Expressions

fringe benefit			附加福利
personnel	/ˌpɜːsəˈnel/	n.	[总称]人员,职员
relocate	/ˌriːləʊˈkeɪt/	v.	搬家;调

Activities

(1) Try to use your own words to explain what you have seen in the video.

(2) What do you think of a job interview?

(3) What do you think are the most important things for you to learn in this job interview? Why?

2. Listen to the following short dialogues and fill in the blanks with the information you get from the tape. Each dialogue will be read twice.

(1) M: Hi, I'm calling about your ad in the paper for the _____ of waiter.

W: Please send us your _____, "Attention: Betty Sue."

(2) M: When can you come in for an _____?

W: Is _____ morning OK with you?

(3) M: What kind of work-related _____ do you have?

W: Well, I worked for ten years as a manager at my _____ company.

(4) M: Would you be willing to work _____?

W: Yes, I am _____ to.

(5) M: Do you have any other _____ about the job?

W: Yes, please tell me about the _____ time.

(6) M: May I ask why you left the _____?

W: I did not think there was any _____ for me to get promoted.

3. You will hear 5 recorded questions. Listen carefully and choose the proper answer to each question. The questions will be spoken twice.

(1) A. A little. B. 45.
   C. As much as. D. As soon as.

(2) A. Of course. B. That's great.
   C. The number is 6544-7086. D. I know what you mean.

(3) A. Susan is a lady. B. Susan is a baby.
   C. Susan is a middle school student. D. Susan is a woman.

(4) A. Is the office big enough for a desk?
   B. Is it a very big office?
   C. Is there room in the office for one more desk?
   D. Is the desk too big to be put in the office?

(5) A. Tell me if you want some help. B. I don't think I can help you.
   C. Do you know where I can get help? D. Let me tell you what I know.

Part III Passages

1. Listen to the passage and supply the missing words. It will be read three times.

1   Good morning, students. Welcome to the _____. I'd like to begin with some information about student housing.

2   First of all, I hope you're getting settled into your new surroundings without too much _____. I know that several of you have moved into our new unit for

single students. It's located on the west side of campus. In this building, four students share a dining and living room, _____, bathroom, and four single bedrooms. We do have a few more empty rooms, so if you're interested in moving in, let me know right away.

3   If you haven't visited the _____ student housing complex, be sure to go and take a look at it. This small community has two-bedroom unfurnished apartments. They are on the south side of campus, near the bus stop for the town center. All apartments are full now, and we have a waiting list for next year. Come and see me if you want to add your name to the list. You should apply as soon as possible for next year.

4   If you want to live off _____ and are still looking for a house, be sure to check out the off-campus housing office. You'll find a lot of rentals listed there.

2. Listen to the passage again and answer the following questions.

(1) Who is the speaker addressing?

(2) How many students can live in one unit?

(3) What does the speaker require those who are interested in the units for single students to do?

(4) What is the speaker's request to those who might move into the family housing complex?

(5) What does the speaker ask those who want to live off campus to do?

3. Listen to the passage and decide whether the following statements are true (T) or false (F).

___ (1) People usually try to make others feel nervous and worried.

___ (2) Men shake hands, but usually only when they are introduced.

___ (3) When women are introduced to each other, they usually don't shake hands.

___ (4) When a woman and a man are introduced, shaking hands is up to the man.

___ (5) On business occasions, Americans usually just shake hands.

4. Watch the video and enjoy the movie clip.

New Words

indispensable	/ˌɪndɪsˈpensəbl/	a.	不可缺少的
statistics	/stəˈtɪstɪks/	n.	统计资料
chronic	/ˈkrɒnɪk/	a.	慢性的,延续很长时间的
indigestion	/ˌɪndɪˈdʒestʃən/	a.	消化不良

Part IV Oral Practice

Text A

Zhang is a graduate. He is having an interview with the personnel manager.

Manager: Good morning. Please sit down. Now I'm going to start off by asking you a few questions. First, I'd like to know something about your educational background, Mr. Zhang. You were an English major, weren't you?

Zhang: Yes, that's right. I've graduated from college for two years.

Manager: Fine. It seems that you are looking for a new job. Could you tell me what kind of work experience you've had?

Zhang: My last position was with Bell Company in Shanghai from 1999 to 2001. And I've been doing freelance work for the last few months.

Manager: From what you've just said, your qualifications for the job are excellent. Could you tell me what kind of salary you are expecting?

Zhang: Personally, I'd much rather have an interesting, a stimulating job with average wages. 5,000 yuan would be fine with me.

Manager: And is there anything you'd like to ask about the job?

Zhang: Yes, I'd like to know if the company provides opportunities of further education.

Manager: Yes, our employees are allowed to take up six hours a week at full pay, to attend additional college courses. Is there anything else you'd like to know?

Zhang: That sounds very encouraging. Besides I wonder whether there are exercises and recreational facilities in the company.

Manager: Sure. We have a gym, a swimming pool and a tennis court.

Text B

Manager: Good afternoon, Mr. Brown. Welcome to our company.

Wu: I want a job in which I can use Japanese. I would also like to be able to have some responsibility in my work.

Manager: I can appreciate that. I would expect my secretary to be able to work under pressure and take over some of my ordinary responsibilities such as answering and routing correspondence and sometimes assisting me with personal business affairs.

Wu: I see. In my previous job, I did the same kind of work.

Manager: Have you had any experience as a guide?

Wu: Well, not exactly, but I have shown some of my foreign friends around Guangzhou and I travelled abroad several times.

Manager: We have visitors from abroad sometimes and I would like to be able to ask my secretary to take them shopping and sightseeing.

Wu: I think I would like to do that.

Manager: I see. Do you have any questions you'd like to ask me about the job?

Wu: Yes, I'd like to ask about the salary. How is it determined?

Manager: Well, new secretary begins at a standard salary of 2500 yuan per month. Based on secretary's performance, it will be adjusted at the end of each year. Any more questions?

Wu: No, Thanks.

Manager: How do you feel about the job?

Wu: I think it sounds like what I am looking for.

Manager: Thank you. You should be hearing from us within five days.

Wu: Thank you.

New Words and Expressions

personnel	/ˌpɜːsəˈnel/	n.	人事部门
freelance	/ˈfriːlæns/	n.	自由作家,自由记者
qualification	/ˌkwɔlɪfɪˈkeɪʃən/	n.	资格,条件
stimulating	/ˈstɪmjuleɪtɪŋ/	a.	刺激的,有刺激性的
recreational	/ˌrekrɪˈeɪʃənəl/	a.	休养的,娱乐的
gym	/dʒɪm/	n.	体育馆,体操
appreciate	/əˈpriːʃɪeɪt/	n.	了解并欣赏
correspondence	/ˌkɔrɪsˈpɔndəns/	n.	通信

Proper Names

Bell Company   贝尔公司

Task   Role Play

Students act as Zhang and Manager or Wu and Manager. Act out Text A or Text B.

Exercises

(1) Imagine you are having a job interview. Make up a dialogue between a personnel manager and yourself. The patterns you learned just now and the vocabulary given below may be of some help to you.

Useful Expressions

personal history	个人资料
job interview	面试
personnel manager	人事经理
qualification	资格, 能力
employer	雇主
employee	雇员
work experience	工作经历

(2) Imagine you are an applicant asking for a job. You want to get some advice from your teacher before a job interview or from an interviewee applying to a computer company for a job. Please make up a dialogue.

Part V Learn to Sing a Song

1. Listen to the song "Right Here Waiting."

2. Listen to the song again and fill in the missing words.

Right Here Waiting

_____ apart day after day, and I slowly go insane.
I hear your voice on the line, but it doesn't stop the pain.
If I see you next to never, how can we say forever.
Wherever you go, whatever you do, I will be right here waiting for you.
Whatever it takes, or how my heart breaks, I will be right here waiting for you.

I took for granted, all the times that I thought would last somehow.
I hear the _____. I taste the tears. But I can't get near you now.
Oh, can't you see it, baby. You've got me going crazy.
Wherever you go, whatever you do, I will be right here waiting for you.
Whatever it takes, or how my heart _____, I will be right here waiting for you.

I wonder how we can survive this romance, but in the end if I'm with you,
I'll take the chance.
Oh, can't you see it baby.
You've got me goin' _____.
Wherever you go, whatever you do,
I will be right here _____ for you.
Whatever it takes or how my heart breaks,
I will be right here waiting for you.

3. Learn to sing the song after the singer.

Vocabulary

符号说明：达到《高职高专教育英语课程教学基本要求》B 级应掌握的词汇：★
达到《高职高专教育英语课程教学基本要求》A 级应掌握的词汇：▲
大学英语 4~6 级词汇：♨

A

	a girl selling flower		卖花女	Unit 4
	a great variety of		各种各样	Unit 4
	a little bit		一点	Unit 3
♨	abbey	/'æbɪ/	n.	修道院；[总称]修道士	Unit 1
♨	absolutely	/'æbsəluːtlɪ/	ad.	完全地，绝对地	Unit 2
★	activity	/æk'tɪvɪtɪ/	n.	行动，活动	Unit 5
♨	allergic	/ə'ləːdʒɪk/	a.	[医]过敏的，患过敏症的	Unit 3
★	America	/ə'merɪkə/		美国；美洲	Unit 3
	Angela	/'ændʒɪlə/	n.	安吉拉（女士名）	Unit 2
♨	anon. = anonymous	/ə'nɒnɪməs/	a.	作者不详的，无名的，佚名的	Unit 5
★	appreciate	/ə'priːʃɪeɪt/	n.	了解并欣赏	Unit 8
▲	approach	/ə'prəʊtʃ/	v.	靠近，接近；动手处理	Unit 3
♨	archeologists	/ˌɑːkɪ'ɒlədʒɪst/	n.	考古学家	Unit 1
	area code			电话地区号	Unit 5
▲	arrow	/'ærəʊ/	n.	箭；箭头记号	Unit 2
	as a matter of fact			事实上	Unit 7
	as long as			只要	Unit 2
★	attractive	/ə'træktɪv/	a.	引人注目的	Unit 4
♨	awareness	/ə'weənɪs/	n.	意识	Unit 7

106

B

★ bare	/bɛə/	a.	赤裸的,无遮蔽的,空的		Unit 1
		v.	使赤裸,露出		Unit 1
be interested in			对……感兴趣		Unit 4
be made of			由……制成		Unit 4
Bell Company			贝尔公司		Unit 8
★ Bill	/bɪl/		比尔(男子名,William 的昵称)		Unit 2
Boston	/'bɔstən/		波士顿(美国马萨诸塞州首府)		Unit 6
Brown	/braʊn/		布朗(姓氏)		Unit 1
★ block	/blɔk/	n.	街区		Unit 4
★ blouse	/blaʊz/	n.	女式衬衣		Unit 4
boarding pass (=boarding card)			登机卡		Unit 3
♨ bookstore	/'bʊkstɔː(r)/	n.	书店		Unit 4
♨ bountiful	/'baʊntɪful/	a.	慷慨的		Unit 7
♨ brass	/brɑːs/	n.	黄铜		Unit 3
▲ breathe	/briːð/	v.	呼吸		Unit 2
♨ bride	/braɪd/	n.	新娘		Unit 6
burn up			燃烧起来		Unit 7
♨ butler	/'bʌtlə/	n.	仆役长,男管家		Unit 1
by the way			顺便说一下		Unit 1

C

Can I help you?			我能帮你吗?		Unit 3
★ ceremony	/'serɪmənɪ/	n.	典礼,仪式,礼节		Unit 6
♨ chronic	/'krɔnɪk/	a.	慢性的,延续很长时间的		Unit 8
Chongqing Electronics Polytechnic College			重庆电子职业技术学院		Unit 1
Claire	/klɛə/		克莱尔(女子名)		Unit 6
▲ client	/'klaɪənt/	n.	顾客,客户		Unit 5
♨ clinic	/'klɪnɪk/	n.	诊所,门诊部,临床		Unit 7
▲ colleague	/'kɔliːg/	n.	同事,同僚		Unit 1
come across			碰到		Unit 3
♨ comely	/'kʌmlɪ/	a.	清秀的,标致的		Unit 5
▲ commercial	/kə'məːʃəl/	a.	商业的		Unit 2
★ complain	/kəm'pleɪn/	v.	抱怨,控诉		Unit 5
★ complete	/kəm'pliːt/	a.	全部的,完全的		Unit 5

▲ complicated	/ˈkɔmplɪkeɪtɪd/	a.	复杂的	Unit 2
▲ conference	/ˈkɔnfərəns/	n.	会议	Unit 2
♨ congressman	/ˈkɔŋgresmən/	n.	国会议员	Unit 5
▲ conservative	/kənˈsəːvətɪv/	a.	保守的	Unit 4
★ constant	/ˈkɔnstənt/	a.	不变的,持续的,坚决的	Unit 5
♨ convent	/ˈkɔnvənt/	n.	女修道会,女修道院	Unit 1
▲ correspondence	/ˌkɔrɪsˈpɔndəns/	n.	通信	Unit 8
★ corridor	/ˈkɔrɪdɔː/	n.	走廊	Unit 2
★ cost	/kɔst/	v.	(使)花费(金钱,时间,劳力等)	Unit 5
★ cough	/kɔːf/	n.	咳嗽	
		v.	咳嗽	Unit 7
♨ crane	/kreɪn/	n.	鹤	Unit 4
♨ creep	/kriːp/	v.	爬,蹑手蹑脚,蔓延	Unit 1
♨ crept	/krept/		(creep 的过去式)	Unit 1
♨ cuff	/kʌf/	n.	袖口	Unit 2

D

★ dare	/dɛə/	v.	敢	Unit 2
★ date	/deɪt/	v.	约会,定日期	Unit 3
Dan	/dæn/		丹(男子名,Daniel 的昵称)	Unit 6
▲ decay	/dɪˈkeɪ/	v. & n.	腐朽,腐烂;衰减	Unit 7
decayed tooth			虫牙,龋齿	Unit 7
♨ decorum	/dɪˈkɔːrəm/	n.	礼貌	Unit 1
♨ decree	/dɪˈkriː/	n.	法令,教令;天命;判决	Unit 6
★ dentist	/ˈdentɪst/	n.	牙科医生	Unit 7
♨ depict	/dɪˈpɪkt/	v.	描述,描写	Unit 1
♨ diaper	/ˈdaɪəpə/	n.	尿布	Unit 3
★ direction	/dɪˈrekʃən/	n.	方向	Unit 2
▲ disaster	/dɪˈzɑːstə/	n.	灾难	Unit 5
▲ discipline	/ˈdɪsɪplɪn/	n.	纪律;学科	Unit 1
★ dream	/driːm/	v.	梦想	Unit 2
♨ dressy	/ˈdresɪ/	a.	衣着考究的	Unit 2
▲ drill	/drɪl/	v.	训练;钻孔;条播(种子)	Unit 1
♨ druggist	/ˈdrʌgɪst/	n.	药剂师,药材商	Unit 7

E

earn	/ɜːn/	v.	赚,挣得,获得		Unit 5
election	/ɪˈlekʃən/	n.	选举		Unit 2
Elizabeth	/ɪˈlɪzəbəθ/		伊丽莎白		Unit 6
embroidered	/ɪmˈbrɔɪdəd/	a.	刺绣的		Unit 4
employee			雇员		Unit 8
employer			雇主		Unit 8
engrave	/ɪnˈgreɪv/	v.	雕刻;使铭记		Unit 6
envy	/ˈenvɪ/	n.	嫉妒,羡慕		Unit 8
escape	/ɪsˈkeɪp/	v.	逃跑,逃避		Unit 7
examine	/ɪgˈzæmɪn/	v.	检查,调查,考试		Unit 7
Excuse me.			劳驾 / 对不起。		Unit 1
exhibition	/ˌeksɪˈbɪʃən/	n.	展览会		Unit 2
exigency	/ˈeksɪdʒənsɪ/	n.	苛求;紧急,紧急事件		Unit 6

F

fashionable	/ˈfæʃənəbl/	a.	时髦的,流行的		Unit 4
fear	/fɪə/	v.	害怕,畏惧		Unit 4
fever	/ˈfiːvə/	n.	发烧,发热		
		v.	(使)发烧		Unit 7
fight	/faɪt/	v.	打架,对抗		Unit 4
fill a tooth			补牙		Unit 7
fingerprint	/ˈfɪŋgəprɪnt/	n.	指纹,手印		
		v.	采指纹		Unit 7
fit	/fɪt/	v.	适合		Unit 4
flower	/ˈflaʊə/	n.	花		Unit 4
follow	/ˈfɔləʊ/	v.	跟随		Unit 2
forgive	/fəˈgɪv/	v.	原谅,饶恕		Unit 7
fray	/freɪ/	v.	使磨损		Unit 2
freelance	/ˈfriːlæns/	n.	自由作家,自由记者		Unit 8
freeze	/friːz/	v.	(使)结冰,(使)冷冻,冻结		Unit 1
freshman	/ˈfreʃmən/	n.	新生,大学一年级学生		Unit 1
fringe benefit			附加福利		Unit 8
funerary	/ˈfjuːnərərɪ/	a.	葬礼的,埋葬的		Unit 1

| ★ fur | /fɜː/ | n. | 毛皮 | Unit 5 |

G

★ glow	/gləʊ/	v.	发光；发热	Unit 6
going-away present			离别礼物	Unit 6
♨ golf	/gɒlf/	n.	高尔夫(球)	Unit 6
♨ gonna	/ˈgɒnə/		[美] (=going to)将要	Unit 3
Good luck!			祝你好运！	Unit 2
♨ gotta	/ˈgɒtə/		[美俚] (=have got to)必须	Unit 3
♨ governess	/ˈgʌvənɪs/	n.	女家庭教师	Unit 1
♨ grace	/greɪs/	n.	优美，雅致，优雅	Unit 5
Green	/griːn/		格林(姓氏)	Unit 2
★ guard	/gɑːd/	n.	哨兵，门卫	Unit 7
guest room			会客室	Unit 2
♨ gum	/gʌm/	n.	牙龈；橡胶；口香糖	Unit 7
▲ gym	/dʒɪm/	n.	体育馆，体操	Unit 8

H

♨ hairdresser	/ˈheədresə(r)/	n.	理发师	Unit 4
★ hall	/hɔːl/	n.	大厅	Unit 2
♨ Halloween	/ˌhæləʊˈiːn/	n.	万圣节前夕，诸圣日前夕	Unit 6
★ handkerchief	/ˈhæŋkətʃɪf/	n.	手帕	Unit 4
★ harbor	/ˈhɑːbə/	n.	港口	Unit 6
Harrison Park			哈理森公园	Unit 6
have the prescriptions filled			(按处方)配药；抓药	Unit 7
★ headache	/ˈhedeɪk/	n.	头痛，令人头痛之事	Unit 7
health record			健康记录	Unit 7
Hear, hear!			说吧，让我们听一听！(这种表达含有赞同的意思。)	Unit 6
★ Hello!			你好！	Unit 1
★ hide	/haɪd/	v.	隐藏，躲藏	Unit 6
♨ holy	/ˈhəʊlɪ/	a.	神圣的，圣洁的	Unit 6
★ host	/həʊst/	n.	主人	
		v.	当主人招待	Unit 6
How do you do?			你好！	Unit 1
How'd it go?= How was it?			怎么样啦？	Unit 6

110

♨ humdinger	/ˈhʌmdɪŋə(r)/	n.		[美俚] 极出色的人(或事物)	Unit 6
♨ humiliating	/hjuːˈmɪlieɪtɪŋ/	a.		羞辱性的	Unit 1
♨ hump	/hʌmp/	n.		驼峰,驼背;小圆丘,峰丘	Unit 1
♨ hurricane	/ˈhʌrɪkən, -kɪn/	n.		飓风,暴风,台风	Unit 6

I

♨ impulse	/ˈɪmpʌls/	n.	推动,推动力;刺激;冲动	Unit 1
in all			总计	Unit 4
in this mess			陷于窘境;一团乱	Unit 7
♨ incorrigible	/ɪnˈkɔrɪdʒəbl/	a.	无药可救的,不能被纠正的	Unit 1
★ independent	/ˌɪndɪˈpendənt/	a.	独立自主的,不受约束的	Unit 6
♨ indigestion	/ˌɪndɪˈdʒestʃən/	a.	消化不良	Unit 8
♨ indispensable	/ˌɪndɪsˈpensəbl/	a.	不可缺少的	Unit 8
★ inquiry	/ɪnˈkwaɪərɪ/	n.	调查	Unit 5
▲ intelligent	/ɪnˈtelɪdʒənt/	a.	聪明的	Unit 2
♨ intern	/ɪnˈtəːn/	n.	实习医师	
		v.	作实习医师	Unit 7
International Conference and Exhibition Center			国际会展中心	Unit 2
It's a pleasure to meet you.			很高兴见到你。	Unit 1
It's a pleasure.			很荣幸。	Unit 3
It's nice to meet you.			很高兴见到你。	Unit 1
I'd like you to meet...			我想请你见见……	Unit 1
I'm wondering if...			我想是否……	Unit 3

J

♨ jail	/dʒeɪl/	n.	监狱	Unit 7
♨ jerk	/dʒəːk/	n.	性情古怪的人	Unit 5
job interview			面试	Unit 8
John	/dʒɔn/		约翰	Unit 6
★ judge	/dʒʌdʒ/	n.	法官,裁判员,鉴赏家	Unit 6

K

Katrina	/kəˈtriːnə/	n.	卡特里娜(女士名)	Unit 2
Kay	/keɪ/		凯(女子名)	Unit 6
Keats	/kiːts/		济慈(1795—1821,英国诗人)	Unit 2

♨ kinda	/ˈkaɪndə/	ad.	(=kind of)有一点,有几分	Unit 3
♨ kiwi	/ˈkiːwiː/	n.	[植]猕猴桃	Unit 3
know one's way around			熟悉周围环境	Unit 2

L

♨ label	/ˈleɪbl/	n.	标签	Unit 2
♨ lawful	/ˈlɔːfəl/	a.	法律许可的,守法的	Unit 6
leave alone			不打搅……	Unit 2
♨ leftover	/ˈleftˌoʊvə/	n.	剩余物	Unit 6
♨ legally	/ˈliːgəlɪ/	a.	法律上,合法地	Unit 6
♨ lime	/laɪm/	n.	酸橙	Unit 3
★ live	/lɪv/	v.	过着,度过,经历	Unit 2
Liverpool Mercury			《利物浦信使报》	Unit 2
♨ lobster	/ˈlɔbstə/	n.	龙虾	Unit 3
▲ locate	/ləʊˈkeɪt/	v.	坐落于	Unit 2
look forward to (doing) sth.			期望,期待,盼望(做)某事	Unit 6
lose the sight of both eyes			双目失明	Unit 4
★ loud	/laʊd/	a.	过分鲜艳的,俗气的	Unit 4

M

▲ maintain	/meinˈteɪn/	v.	维持;继续;供养;主张	Unit 1
★ major	/ˈmeɪdʒə/	v.	主修	Unit 1
major in			主修,专攻	Unit 1
marketing manager			市场营销部经理	Unit 1
Mary	/ˈmɛrɪ/		玛丽(女子名)	Unit 1
New York			纽约	Unit 3
▲ mask	/mɑːsk/	n.	面具	
		v.	戴面具,掩饰	Unit 7
♨ matrimony	/ˈmætrɪmənɪ/	n.	结婚	Unit 6
Ma'am	/mæm/		= Madam /ˈmædəm/	Unit 3
medical insurance			医疗保险	Unit 7
★ model	/ˈmɔdl/	n.	模特	Unit 4
♨ moody	/ˈmuːdɪ/	a.	喜怒无常的,忧悒的	Unit 3
♨ mourning	/ˈmɔːnɪŋ/	n.	悲恸,服丧	Unit 1
★ musician	/mjuːˈzɪʃən/	n.	音乐家	Unit 4
My name is...			我叫……	Unit 1

N

★ nephew	/ˈnefjʊ(ː)/	n.	侄子,外甥	Unit 3
nice-looking	/ˈnaɪsˈlʊkɪŋ/	a.	好看的	Unit 4
★ niece	/niːs/	n.	侄女	Unit 6
not in the mood			(没)有心情	Unit 5
♨ nuts	/nʌts/	a.	[美俚] 热衷的,发狂的	Unit 3

O

♨ oak	/əʊk/	n.	橡树	Unit 2
on business			(因公)出差	Unit 1
Opal	/ˈəʊpəl/		奥珀尔(女子名)	Unit 6
★ operator	/ˈɔpəreɪtə/	n.	(电话)接线员	Unit 5
★ opportunity	/ˌɔpəˈtjuːnɪtɪ/	n.	机会	Unit 5
★ opposite	/ˈɔpəzɪt/	a.	对面的	Unit 2
out of line			不成直线,不协调	Unit 5

P

pain-killer			止痛药	Unit 7
★ painter	/ˈpeɪntə/	n.	画家	Unit 4
♨ pajamas	/pəˈdʒɑːməz/	n.	睡衣	Unit 2
▲ palm	/pɑːm/	n.	手掌	Unit 4
♨ parasol	/ˌpærəˈsɔl, ˈpærəsɔl/	n.	(女用)阳伞	Unit 1
★ part	/pɑːt/	v.	分开	Unit 2
★ partner	/ˈpɑːtnə/	n.	合伙人,股东	Unit 1
♨ password	/ˈpɑːswɜːd/	n.	密码,口令	Unit 5
★ perfect	/ˈpɜːfɪkt/	a.	极好的	Unit 6
♨ persevere	/ˌpɜːsɪˈvɪə/	v.	坚持不懈;坚韧	Unit 8
personal history			个人资料	Unit 8
★ personnel	/ˌpɜːsəˈnel/	n.	[总称]人员,职员	Unit 8
★ personnel	/ˌpɜːsəˈnel/	n.	人事部门	Unit 8
Personnel Department			人事部	Unit 2
personnel manager			人事经理	Unit 8
♨ perspective	/pəˈspektɪv/	n.	透视图,远景,观察	Unit 5
Peter	/ˈpiːtə/		彼得(男子名)	Unit 6

pharaoh	/ˈfɛərəu/	n.	法老(古埃及君主称号),暴君	Unit 1
photocopier	/ˈfəutəukɔpɪə(r)/	n.	复印机	Unit 5
★ pie	/paɪ/	n.	馅饼	Unit 3
pleasing	/ˈpliːzɪŋ/	a.	令人高兴的,愉快的,合意的	Unit 5
▲ prescribe	/prɪsˈkraɪb/	v.	指示,规定,处(方),开(药)	Unit 7
▲ prescription	/prɪˈskrɪpʃən/	n.	指示,命令,处方,药方	Unit 7
presume	/prɪˈzjuːm/	v.	假定,假设,认为	Unit 1
▲ primitive	/ˈprɪmɪtɪv/	a.	原始的,远古的;粗糙的;简单的	Unit 1
★ prison	/ˈprɪzn/	v.	监禁;紧紧抱住	Unit 7
★ pronounce	/prəˈnauns/	v.	发音,宣告,断言	Unit 6
★ property	/ˈprɔpəti/	n.	财产,所有物	Unit 5
pull out a tooth			拔牙	Unit 7
purple	/ˈpəːpl/	a.	紫色的	Unit 3
put sb. through			使某人经受,遭受	Unit 7
★ puzzle	/ˈpʌzl/	v.	使迷惑	Unit 2

Q

QQ	/ˈkjuːkjuː/	n.	一种即时互动通信软件	Unit 5
qualification	/ˌkwɔlɪfɪˈkeɪʃən/	n.	资格,条件	Unit 8

R

radiance	/ˈreɪdɪəns/	n.	光辉	Unit 7
ragged	/ˈrægɪd/	a.	破烂的,粗糙的	Unit 4
ramble	/ˈræmbl/	v.	漫游,漫步	Unit 6
★ reasonable	/ˈriːznəbl/	a.	合理的,公道的	Unit 4
▲ receptionist	/reˈsepʃənɪst/	n.	招待员,接话员	Unit 5
★ recognize	/ˈrekəgnaɪz/	v.	认识,认出	Unit 4
★ recommendation	/ˌrekəmenˈdeɪʃən/	n.	推荐,介绍(信)	Unit 5
recreational	/ˌrekrɪˈeɪʃənl/	a.	休养的,娱乐的	Unit 8
★ register	/ˈredʒɪstə/	v.	登记,注册	Unit 5
rejoin	/ˌriːˈdʒɔɪn/	v.	再次加入	Unit 6
relocate	/ˌriːləuˈkeɪt/	v.	搬家;调	Unit 8
remove the tartar from your teeth			去除牙石	Unit 7
rent	/rent/	v.	租,租借	Unit 5

♨ romantic	/rəʊˈmæntɪk/	a.	浪漫的	Unit 4
run away from			摆脱	Unit 2

S

♨ sate	/seɪt/	v.	使心满意足,过分地给与	Unit 1
★ say	/seɪ/	v.	假设	Unit 6
★ scratch	/skrætʃ/	n.	抓痕;擦伤	
		v.	擦,刮	Unit 7
★ scream	/skriːm/	v.	尖叫,吼叫	Unit 7
self-seeking	/ˌselfˈsiːkɪŋ/	a.	追求私利的	Unit 8
★ sell	/sel/	v.	卖	Unit 4
★ serve	/sɜːv/	v.	服务,侍候	Unit 4
♨ sexy	/ˈseksɪ/	a.	性感的	Unit 2
★ shoot	/ʃuːt/	v.	拍摄	Unit 3
short message			短消息	Unit 5
show sb. sth.			把……给……看	Unit 4
★ sight	/saɪt/	n.	视力,视线	Unit 2
▲ signature	/ˈsɪgnɪtʃə/	n.	签名	Unit 5
★ silk	/sɪlk/	n.	丝绸	Unit 4
★ silver	/ˈsɪlvə/	n.	银,银器	Unit 4
Sohpia			苏菲亚	Unit 3
So now I'm taking a flight on Moday instead.			所以我现在准备改搭星期一的班机走。	Unit 6
▲ sophisticated	/səˈfɪstɪkeɪtɪd/	a.	诡辩的;久经世故的	Unit 1
sore throat			喉咙痛	Unit 7
★ specific	/spɪˈsɪfɪk/	a.	明确的	Unit 5
♨ spout	/spaʊt/	n.	喷管,喷口,壶嘴	Unit 3
▲ statistics	/stəˈtɪstɪks/	n.	统计资料	Unit 8
▲ stereo	/ˈstɪərɪəʊ/	n.	立体声电唱机	Unit 6
♨ stimulating	/ˈstɪmjʊleɪtɪŋ/	a.	刺激的,有刺激性的	Unit 8
♨ stomachache	/ˈstʌməkeɪk/	n.	胃痛,肚子痛	Unit 7
♨ stout	/staʊt/	a.	结实的,健壮的	Unit 3
▲ stuff	/stʌf/	n.	原料,材料	Unit 5
♨ suitcase	/ˈsjuːtkeɪs/	n.	手提箱,衣箱	Unit 3
♨ super	/ˈsjuːpə/	a.	极好的	Unit 6
▲ supplement	/ˈsʌplɪmənt/	n.	补遗,补充;附录,增刊	Unit 1
★ suppose	/səˈpəʊz/	v.	应该,假设	Unit 6
♨ surge	/sɜːdʒ/	n.	汹涌	Unit 7

115

swarthy	/ˈswɔːðɪ/	a.	黑黝黝的	Unit 4
swiftly	/ˈswɪftlɪ/	ad.	很快地,迅速地;即刻	Unit 2
syllabus	/ˈsɪləbəs/	n.	课程提纲	Unit 1
sympathize with sb.			同情某人	Unit 4

T

tablecloth	/ˈteɪb(ə)lklɔθ/	n.	桌布	Unit 4
tablespoonful	/ˈteɪb(ə)lspuːnfʊl/	n.	一大汤匙的量	Unit 7
take a chance			冒险,碰运气	Unit 2
take the lift			乘电梯	Unit 2
tan	/tæn/	v.	(使)晒成棕褐色	Unit 4
tartar	/ˈtɑːtə/	n.	酒石;[医]牙垢	Unit 7
technician	/tekˈnɪʃ(ə)n/	n.	技术员	Unit 5
temperature	/ˈtemprətʃə(r)/	n.	温度	Unit 7
That's all right.			好的。	Unit 3
the check-in counter			(机场)登记处	Unit 3
the East			(美国)东部	Unit 6
the Friendship Department Store			友谊商店	Unit 4
the People's Park			人民公园	Unit 2
Tom	/tɔm/		汤姆(男子名)	Unit 1
thicken	/ˈθɪkən/	v.	使变厚,使变粗	Unit 4
This way, please.			这边请。	Unit 1
tip	/tɪp/	v.	(使)倾斜	Unit 3
totally	/ˈtəʊt(ə)li/	ad.	完全地,当然	Unit 5
tramp	/træmp/	n.	流浪汉	Unit 4
transfer	/trænsˈfɜː/	v.	换(车)	Unit 2
trolley	/ˈtrɔlɪ/	n.	电车	Unit 2
try one's best to do sth.			尽力做某事	Unit 4
typical	/ˈtɪpɪkəl/	a.	典型的,有代表性的	Unit 4

U

utmost	/ˈʌtməust/	a.	极度的;最远的	Unit 1

V

vendor	/ˈvendɔː/	n.	卖主	Unit 2

vest	/vest/	n.	背心		
		v.	使穿衣服,授予	Unit 6	
vicar	/ˈvɪkə/	n.	教区牧师	Unit 2	

W

	/weɪd/	v.	跋涉		
		n.	跋涉,可涉水而过的地方	Unit 4	
wanna	/ˈwɒnə/	v.	[美俚] (= want to)想要,希望	Unit 3	
We thought alike = We thought the same thought / We shared the same idea				Unit 6	
weary	/ˈwɪərɪ/	a.	厌倦的,令人厌烦的	Unit 4	
wedding	/ˈwedɪŋ/	n.	婚礼,婚宴,结婚典礼	Unit 6	
Welcome to...			欢迎来到……	Unit 1	
Wetland Road			维特兰路	Unit 6	
★ White	/(h)waɪt/		怀特(姓氏)	Unit 1	
What can I do for you?			您要什么？有什么事可以为您效劳？	Unit 4	
What do you think of...?			你认为……怎么样？	Unit 4	
Where are you from?			你从什么地方来？	Unit 1	
whip	/(h)wɪp/	v.	打败,赢,胜过	Unit 6	
wildly	/ˈwaɪldlɪ/	ad.	狂热地,野蛮地	Unit 2	
wintry	/ˈwɪntrɪ/	a.	像冬季的,寒冷的,冬天的,冷淡的	Unit 1	
★ wolf	/wʊlf/	n.	狼	Unit 4	
work experience			工作经历	Unit 8	
Would you like to choose anything else?			还要选点别的吗？	Unit 4	
★ wrong	/rɒŋ/	n.	坏事,恶行	Unit 8	

Y

You are welcome.			不用谢。	Unit 3	

CNN热门话题新闻英语系列

本系列丛书精心选择CNN热门话题,设计编写为一套分三个层次的新闻英语学习丛书。特点:每章三篇选文从不同视角探讨同一个热点话题,文章内容的不同语言不同,逐渐增加文章阐述难度。确保读者参与,刺激思考,引出谈话的热门主题,文章探究的话题对读者而言都不只一个方面,鼓励了辩论和课堂上的互动。通过预备问题,略读和浏览活动,对上下文线索的利用,词汇分析,批判性思考技能的培养,对阅读技巧和阅读理解的集中关注,帮助学生增加新闻阅读的流畅性。

本套丛书作为教材的教师同时可获赠含大量题库的CD-ROM和教学指导录像,更加方便教师组织测验和教学。

热门话题新闻英语(1)	Cheryl Pavlik	定价 22.00
热门话题新闻英语(2)	Cheryl Pavlik	定价 22.00
热门话题新闻英语(3)	Cheryl Pavlik	定价 24.50
热门话题新闻英语指导手册	Cheryl Pavlik	定价 22.00

说得地道社交英语

本书特为提高英语表达技能而编写的社交英语教材。通过讲授各种社交背景和情境的重要英语表达方式,帮助学习者掌握社交英语的表达,自如应对各种日常社交场合,更快地融入社会交往。

说得地道社交英语(1)	Betty Kirkpatrick	定价 22.00
说得地道社交英语(2)	Betty Kirkpatrick	定价 22.00

北京大学出版社

外语编辑部电话:010-62767347 市场营销部电话:010-62750672
　　　　　　　010-62755217   邮 购 部 电 话:010-62752015
Email: zbing@pup.pku.edu.cn